Renal Diet Cookbook for Seniors:

2700 Days of Quick & Healthy Recipes to Manage Kidney Health - With Easy 30-Day Meal Plan

BAILEY LAMBERT

Legal Notice

Disclaimer Notice

Table of Contents

INTRODUCTION

About the Renal Diet

The renal diet is specifically designed to support kidney health by controlling the intake of certain nutrients that can put stress on the kidneys. It is crucial for individuals with compromised kidney function, especially seniors, to maintain a proper balance of nutrients like sodium, potassium, phosphorus, and protein. The main goal of the renal diet is to reduce the workload on the kidneys, helping them to function more efficiently and prevent further damage.

A well-planned renal diet can slow the progression of kidney disease, reduce symptoms, and improve overall well-being. Seniors, in particular, benefit from a renal diet that is easy to digest, nutritionally balanced, and aligned with their specific health needs.

Understanding Kidney Health and Nutrition

The kidneys play a vital role in the body by filtering waste and excess fluids from the blood and balancing electrolytes. When kidney function declines, waste products and fluids can build up, causing health problems. A renal diet focuses on limiting certain nutrients:

- **Sodium**: Excess sodium can lead to fluid retention, swelling, and high blood pressure, which can strain the kidneys.

- **Potassium**: While potassium is essential for heart and muscle function, too much of it can be harmful for those with reduced kidney function.

- **Phosphorus**: High phosphorus levels can weaken bones and lead to heart disease in individuals with kidney disease.

- **Protein**: While protein is important for overall health, excessive intake can burden the kidneys, so moderation is key.

Balancing these nutrients helps to maintain the right levels in the body, ensuring that the kidneys don't have to work harder than necessary. Seniors with chronic kidney disease or at risk of kidney problems should follow this dietary plan to support their kidney function, reduce complications, and maintain a better quality of life.

This cookbook is designed with these principles in mind, offering easy, delicious recipes that help seniors enjoy their meals while supporting kidney health.

Importance of a Renal Diet for Seniors

As we age, kidney function can naturally decline, and many seniors are at an increased risk for developing chronic kidney disease (CKD). Seniors may also face additional challenges such as high blood pressure, diabetes, and heart disease, which further contribute to the strain on the kidneys. A renal diet is essential for slowing the progression of CKD and managing the health issues associated with impaired kidney function.

For seniors, the renal diet plays a crucial role in:

Excess sodium and fluid intake can lead to swelling, high blood pressure, and strain on the heart. A renal diet helps control sodium intake, reducing these risks. Elevated potassium and phosphorus levels can lead to dangerous complications, including heart rhythm issues and bone weakening. The renal diet ensures proper balance of these minerals.

A well-balanced diet tailored to kidney health provides seniors with the necessary energy and nutrients while minimizing the burden on their kidneys. Many seniors with kidney issues also have comorbidities like hypertension or diabetes. The renal diet not only supports kidney health but also helps manage blood pressure, blood sugar, and overall cardiovascular health.

By following a controlled diet, seniors can preserve their remaining kidney function and avoid or delay the need for dialysis or more intensive medical interventions.

This diet is particularly important for seniors because their nutritional needs change with age and maintaining kidney health directly impacts their overall quality of life, mobility, and independence.

How to Use This Cookbook?

This cookbook is specifically designed to make the renal diet easy, enjoyable, and accessible for seniors. It provides a variety of recipes that not only cater to kidney health but also taste great, encouraging long-term adherence to the diet. Here's how to get the most out of this book:

The recipes are organized by **meal types**—breakfast, lunch, dinner, snacks, sides, soups, beverages, and desserts—so you can quickly find the perfect dish for any time of day. Each chapter provides a range of options to suit different tastes and occasions. Each recipe has been crafted to follow renal dietary guidelines, including controlled levels of sodium, potassium, phosphorus, and protein. This allows you to cook worry-free, knowing the recipes are safe for kidney health.

The cookbook includes a **30-day meal plan** to help you, or your loved one gets started on a well-balanced diet. This plan takes the guesswork out of daily meal preparation and helps create a structured routine that supports kidney health.

All recipes are designed to be simple and senior-friendly, using ingredients that are widely available and methods that are straightforward. Many dishes can be prepared in advance or stored for later, making meal preparation easier for seniors or caregivers. Recipes are tailored to suit the needs of seniors, with easy-to-chew ingredients, low preparation times, and simple instructions. Seniors who are managing other health issues like diabetes or hypertension will also benefit from the balanced, nutrient-conscious meals. The bonus chapter provides special, kidney-friendly recipes for holiday gatherings, so seniors can enjoy festive meals without compromising their health.

Feel free to modify recipes to suit personal taste while keeping the key ingredients that maintain the balance for kidney health. Portion sizes can be adjusted depending on individual needs, and additional meal plans can be created using the recipes in the book.

By following the recipes and meal plans in this cookbook, you or your loved one can enjoy delicious, satisfying meals while protecting kidney function and supporting overall health.

Foods to Include and Avoid in a Renal Diet

Maintaining a renal diet means carefully selecting foods that support kidney function while avoiding those that can overburden the kidneys. Here's a breakdown of the types of foods to include and avoid in your daily meals:

Foods to Include

- **Low-Potassium Fruits and Vegetables**:
  Apples, berries (strawberries, blueberries), grapes, pears, pineapples, and peaches. These fruits are low in potassium, making them safer for the kidneys compared to bananas or oranges. Cauliflower, cabbage, zucchini, green beans, carrots, and bell peppers.
- **Lean Proteins and Egg Whites**:
  Chicken, turkey, lean cuts of beef, and fish. Choose fresh, unprocessed, and lean proteins that are lower in phosphorus and sodium.
  Egg whites are a great source of high-quality protein without the phosphorus found in yolks.
- **Rice, Pasta, and Bread**:
  White rice, pasta, and bread contain less potassium and phosphorus than their whole grain counterparts, making them better choices for a renal diet.
- **Unsalted Snacks**:
  Popcorn, rice cakes, and unsalted crackers. Opt for snacks that are low in sodium to prevent fluid retention and hypertension.
- **Herbs and Spices**:
  Basil, parsley, oregano, and garlic (in moderation) can add flavor without the need for added salt.
- **Healthy Fats**: Olive oil, avocado oil (in moderation), and unsaturated fats help to enhance flavor and promote heart health without burdening the kidneys.

Foods to Avoid

- ❖ **High-Potassium Foods**:
  Bananas, oranges, avocados, potatoes, tomatoes, and spinach. These foods are high in potassium, which can build up blood and cause serious complications for those with kidney disease.
- ❖ **High-Phosphorus Foods**:

Dairy products like milk, cheese, yogurt, and processed foods that contain phosphorus additives. Phosphorus can weaken bones and damage blood vessels if consumed in excess by individuals with impaired kidney function.

❖ **High-Sodium Foods**:
Processed meats (bacon, ham, sausages), canned soups, frozen dinners, and snack foods like chips and pretzels. Sodium increases blood pressure and leads to fluid retention, making it a critical nutrient to limit in a renal diet.

❖ **Whole Grains and Bran Products**:
While generally healthy for others, whole grains such as whole wheat bread, brown rice, and bran cereals are higher in potassium and phosphorus, making them less ideal for those on a renal diet.

❖ **Dark-Colored Sodas and Processed Foods**:
Many sodas and processed foods contain hidden phosphorus additives that can harm the kidneys.

❖ **Dairy and Cheese**:
Dairy products are high in phosphorus and potassium, so limit milk, cheese, and other dairy items, substituting them with lower-phosphorus alternatives.

❖ **Nuts and Seeds**:
While nutritious, nuts, seeds, and legumes are often high in both phosphorus and potassium, which need to be limited in a renal diet.

Tips for Grocery Shopping and Meal Planning

Adopting a renal-friendly diet doesn't have to be overwhelming. With thoughtful grocery shopping and meal planning strategies, you can easily stay on track and ensure your meals support kidney health.

Grocery Shopping Tips

Focus on fresh fruits, vegetables, lean meats, and whole foods that are naturally low in sodium, potassium, and phosphorus. Avoid processed and pre-packaged items that often contain hidden salts and additives. Look for items labeled "low-sodium," "no salt added," or "reduced-sodium." Carefully check nutrition labels for hidden potassium, phosphorus, and sodium in ingredients. Phosphorus additives often end in "-phos" on labels.

Keep a list of low-potassium options such as apples, berries, cauliflower, and green beans. These are safe to eat in larger portions and can be used in many meals. Opt for fresh cuts of meat, poultry, and fish over processed options like deli meats, sausages, or pre-marinated products. These are usually high in sodium and preservatives.

Meal Planning Tips

Aim to balance your intake of protein, sodium, potassium, and phosphorus. This cookbook provides recipes that naturally align with these needs, so you can easily mix and match dishes.

Prepare large portions of renal-friendly meals (like soups or casseroles) and store them in the fridge or freezer for easy reheating. This makes it easier to stick to the diet even on busy days. Rotate different recipes throughout the week to prevent meal fatigue. For example, switch between different breakfast options like oatmeal, egg whites, and smoothies to keep things interesting.

Stick to appropriate serving sizes, especially with high-protein or higher-potassium foods. Use a food scale or measuring cups to ensure you're eating the right amounts.

✓ **Stay Hydrated**:

Proper hydration is important for kidney health, but it's essential to follow your doctor's guidelines regarding fluid intake, especially if you're on a fluid-restricted diet.

✓ **Use the 30-Day Meal Plan**:

This cookbook's 30-day meal plan is a helpful guide for starting and maintaining a balanced renal diet. Follow it or use it as inspiration to create your own weekly plans.

✓ **Adapt Recipes to Your Preferences**:

Don't be afraid to modify the recipes based on your personal taste or dietary needs. Just ensure that substitutions remain within the renal diet guidelines.

By following these shopping and meal planning tips, you can make sure your kitchen is stocked with kidney-friendly ingredients, making it easier to prepare nutritious meals that promote better kidney health.

CHAPTER 1
Breakfast Delights

1. Low-Sodium Oatmeal with Berries

Yield: 2 servings | **Prep time**: 5 minutes | **Cook time**: 5 minutes

Ingredients:

- 1 cup rolled oats
- 2 cups of water
- 1/2 cup fresh blueberries
- 1 tablespoon ground flaxseed
- 1 teaspoon cinnamon
- 1 teaspoon honey (optional)

Directions:

1. In a saucepan, bring water to a boil. Add the oats and reduce heat to a simmer. Cook for 5 minutes or until the oats reach your desired consistency.

2. Stir in the ground flaxseed and cinnamon. Mix well.

3. Divide the oatmeal into two bowls and top with fresh blueberries.

4. Drizzle with honey if desired and serve warmth.

Nutritional Information per serving: 180 calories, 5g protein,

32g carbohydrates, 3g total fat,

5g fiber, 0mg cholesterol, 10mg sodium,

160mg potassium, 6g sugars,

235 mg phosphorus.

2. Scrambled Egg Whites with Spinach

Yield: 2 servings | **Prep time**: 5 minutes | **Cook time**: 5 minutes

Ingredients:

- 4 large egg whites
- 1 cup fresh spinach leaves
- 1 tablespoon olive oil
- 1/4 teaspoon black pepper
- 1/4 teaspoon garlic powder

Directions:

1. Heat olive oil in a non-stick pan over medium heat.

2. Add spinach and sauté until it wilted, for about 2 minutes.

3. In a small bowl, whisk the egg whites, black pepper, and garlic powder.

4. Pour the egg white into the pan and scramble with the spinach until fully cooked, for about 3 minutes.

5. Serve hot alongside whole wheat toast or a slice of avocado if desired.

Nutritional Information per serving: 100 calories, 8g protein,

3g carbohydrates, 6g total fat, 1g fiber, 0mg cholesterol, 75mg sodium,

150mg potassium, 0g sugars,

55 mg phosphorus.

3. Fluffy Pancakes with Blueberries

Yield: 4 servings | **Prep time**: 10 minutes | **Cook time**: 10 minutes

Ingredients:

- 1 cup all-purpose flour
- 1 tablespoon baking powder
- 1 tablespoon sugar
- 1 cup almond milk (unsweetened)
- 1 tablespoon olive oil
- 1/2 cup fresh blueberries

Directions:

1. In a large bowl, mix the flour, baking powder, and sugar.

2. In a separate bowl, whisk together almond milk and olive oil.

3. Gradually pour the wet ingredients into the dry ingredients, stirring until just combined.

4. Heat a non-stick skillet over medium heat and lightly grease with oil. Pour 1/4 cup batter into the pan and sprinkle a few blueberries on top.

5. Cook until bubbles form on the surface of the pancake, then flip and cook for another 2 minutes.

Nutritional Information per serving: 150 calories, 3g protein,

28g carbohydrates, 4g total fat, 2g fiber, 0mg cholesterol, 80mg sodium,

180mg potassium, 7g sugars,

85 mg phosphorus.

4. Vegetable Breakfast Muffins

Yield: 6 muffins | **Prep time**: 10 minutes | **Cook time**: 20 minutes

Ingredients:

- 6 large egg whites
- 1/2 cup diced bell peppers
- 1/4 cup of diced onions
- 1/4 cup shredded low-fat cheddar cheese, 1 tablespoon olive oil
- 1/4 teaspoon black pepper, 1/4 teaspoon garlic powder

Directions:

1. Preheat the oven to 350°F (175°C) and lightly grease a muffin tin with olive oil.

2. In a skillet, heat olive oil and sauté bell peppers and onions until soft, for about 3 minutes.

3. In a mixing bowl, whisk the egg whites, black pepper, and garlic powder.

4. Pour the mixture into the muffin tins, filling each cup about 3/4 full.

5. Bake for 15-20 minutes or until the muffins are set and slightly golden on top.

Nutritional Information per muffin:

80 calories, 6g protein,

2g carbohydrates, 5g total fat, 0g fiber, 0mg cholesterol, 70mg sodium,

110mg potassium, 1g sugars,

90 mg phosphorus.

5. Smoothie Bowls with Low-Potassium Fruits

Yield: 2 servings | **Prep time**: 10 minutes | **Cook time**: 0 minutes

Ingredients:

- 1 cup almond milk (unsweetened)
- 1/2 cup frozen strawberries
- 1/2 cup frozen blueberries
- 1/4 cup of oats
- 1 tablespoon chia seeds
- 1/4 cup Greek yogurt (optional)
- 1 tablespoon honey (optional)
- Toppings: fresh berries, sliced apples, and a sprinkle of granola

Directions:

1. In a blender, combine almond milk, frozen strawberries, frozen blueberries, oats, and chia seeds. Blend until smooth.

2. Pour the smoothie into bowls and top with fresh berries, apple slices, and a sprinkle of granola. Add Greek yogurt and honey if desired.

3. Serve immediately.

Nutritional Information per serving: 210 calories, 8g protein,

35g carbohydrates, 5g total fat, 6g fiber, 5mg cholesterol, 65mg sodium,

200mg potassium, 12g sugars,

135 mg phosphorus.

6. Cinnamon-Spiced French Toast

Yield: 2 servings | **Prep time**: 5 minutes | **Cook time**: 10 minutes

Ingredients:

- 4 slices of low-sodium white bread
- 4 large egg whites
- 1/2 cup almond milk
- 1 teaspoon ground cinnamon
- 1/2 teaspoon vanilla extract
- 1 tablespoon olive oil (for cooking)
- Optional toppings: fresh berries, a drizzle of maple syrup

Directions:

1. In a shallow bowl, whisk together egg whites, almond milk, cinnamon, and vanilla extract.

2. Heat olive oil in a non-stick skillet over medium heat. Dip each slice of bread into the egg mixture, coating both sides.

3. Place the bread on the skillet and cook for 2-3 minutes on each side, or until golden brown.

4. Serve warm with optional toppings like fresh berries or a light drizzle of maple syrup.

Nutritional Information per serving: 220 calories, 8g protein,

32g carbohydrates, 6g total fat, 2g fiber, 0mg cholesterol, 120mg sodium,

170mg potassium, 6g sugars,

95 mg phosphorus.

7. Low-Sodium Breakfast Burrito

Yield: 2 servings | **Prep time**: 10 minutes | **Cook time**: 10 minutes

Ingredients:

- 4 large egg whites
- 1/4 cup of diced onions, diced bell peppers and low-fat shredded cheddar cheese
- 2 low-sodium whole wheat tortillas, 1 tablespoon olive oil
- 1/4 teaspoon black pepper, garlic powder

Directions:

1. Heat olive oil in a non-stick pan and sauté onions and bell peppers until soft, about 3-4 minutes.

2. In a bowl, whisk the egg whites with black pepper and garlic powder. Add to the skillet and scramble until fully cooked, about 3 minutes.

3. Remove from heat and divide the egg mixture between the two tortillas. Sprinkle each with cheddar cheese.

4. Fold the sides of the tortillas and roll them into burritos. Serve warm with salsa.

Nutritional Information per serving: 240 calories, 18g protein,

22g carbohydrates, 9g total fat, 3g fiber, 0mg cholesterol, 150mg sodium,

250mg potassium, 4g sugars,

170 mg phosphorus.

8. Apple Cinnamon Quinoa Porridge

Yield: 2 servings | **Prep time**: 5 minutes | **Cook time**: 15 minutes

Ingredients:

- 1/2 cup quinoa, rinsed
- 1 cup of water
- 1/2 cup almond milk (unsweetened)
- 1 small apple, diced
- 1 teaspoon ground cinnamon
- 1 tablespoon honey (optional)

Directions:

1. In a saucepan, bring water to a boil. Add quinoa, reduce heat to a simmer, and cook for 12-15 minutes or until tender.

2. Stir in almond milk, diced apple, and cinnamon. Cook for another 2-3 minutes until the mixture thickens and the apples soften.

3. Drizzle with honey if desired and serve warmth.

Nutritional Information per serving: 220 calories, 6g protein,

40g carbohydrates, 4g total fat, 5g fiber, 0mg cholesterol, 10mg sodium,

230mg potassium, 12g sugars,

210 mg phosphorus.

9. Egg White Frittata with Bell Peppers

Yield: 2 servings | **Prep time**: 10 minutes | **Cook time**: 15 minutes

Ingredients:

- 6 large egg whites
- 1/2 cup diced bell peppers (red, green, or yellow)
- 1/4 cup of diced onions, 1/4 teaspoon black pepper and 1/4 teaspoon garlic powder, 1/4 cup low-fat shredded cheddar cheese.
- 1 tablespoon olive oil

Directions:

1. Preheat the oven to 350°F (175°C).
2. In an oven-safe skillet, heat olive oil over medium heat. Sauté bell peppers and onions until softened, about 5 minutes.
3. In a bowl, whisk the egg whites, black pepper, and garlic powder. Pour the mixture over the sautéed vegetables.
4. Cook on the stove for 2-3 minutes until the edges start to set. Sprinkle with cheese if desired. Transfer the skillet to the oven and bake for 8-10 minutes.

Nutritional Information per serving: 140 calories, 10g protein,

6g carbohydrates, 7g total fat, 2g fiber, 0mg cholesterol, 80mg sodium,

190mg potassium, 2g sugars,

120 mg phosphorus.

10. Cranberry and Apple Chia Pudding

Yield: 2 servings | **Prep time**: 5 minutes | **Cook time**: 0 minutes (overnight refrigeration)

Ingredients:

- 1 cup almond milk (unsweetened)
- 2 tablespoons chia seeds
- 1/4 cup diced apple
- 2 tablespoons of dried cranberries (unsweetened)
- 1/2 teaspoon cinnamon
- 1 tablespoon honey (optional)

Directions:

1. In a bowl, whisk together almond milk, chia seeds, cinnamon, and honey.
2. Stir in the diced apple and cranberries.
3. Cover the bowl and refrigerate for at least 4 hours, or overnight, until the chia seeds have absorbed the liquid and thickened into a pudding.
4. Serve chilled, topped with extra apple slices if desired.

Nutritional Information per serving: 180 calories, 4g protein,

30g carbohydrates, 6g total fat, 9g fiber, 0mg cholesterol, 40mg sodium,

180mg potassium, 15g sugars,

130 mg phosphorus

11. Renal-Friendly Breakfast Sandwiches

Yield: 2 servings | **Prep time**: 5 minutes | **Cook time**: 10 minutes

Ingredients:

- 4 large egg whites
- 2 slices of low-sodium whole wheat bread
- 1/4 cup low-fat shredded cheddar cheese
- 1/4 avocado, sliced
- 1 tablespoon olive oil
- 1/4 teaspoon black pepper

Directions:

1. Heat olive oil in a non-stick skillet. Scramble the egg whites with black pepper until fully cooked.

2. Toast the bread slices in a toaster.

3. Assemble the sandwich by placing the scrambled egg whites on one slice of bread, topping with shredded cheese and avocado slices, and then covering with the second slice of bread.

4. Serve immediately, optionally with a side of fresh fruit.

Nutritional Information per serving: 250 calories, 15g protein,

20g carbohydrates, 12g total fat,

3g fiber, 0mg cholesterol, 120mg sodium, 250mg potassium, 3g sugars,

190 mg phosphorus.

12. Warm Cinnamon Rice Cereal

Yield: 2 servings | **Prep time**: 5 minutes | **Cook time**: 10 minutes

Ingredients:

- 1/2 cup white rice
- 1 1/2 cups of water
- 1/2 cup almond milk (unsweetened)
- 1 teaspoon ground cinnamon
- 1 tablespoon honey (optional)
- 1/4 teaspoon vanilla extract

Directions:

1. In a saucepan, bring water to a boil. Add the rice and reduce heat to a simmer. Cover and cook for 10 minutes or until the rice is tender.

2. Stir in the almond milk, cinnamon, honey, and vanilla extract. Cook for another 2 minutes until the mixture is creamy and warmed through.

3. Serve warm, optionally topped with fresh berries or a sprinkle of cinnamon.

Nutritional Information per serving: 180 calories, 4g protein,

35g carbohydrates, 3g total fat, 1g fiber, 0mg cholesterol, 10mg sodium,

130mg potassium, 7g sugars,

80 mg phosphorus.

13. Greek Yogurt Parfait with Strawberries

Yield: 2 servings | **Prep time**: 5 minutes | **Cook time**: 0 minutes

Ingredients:

- 1 cup plain, low-fat Greek yogurt
- 1/2 cup fresh strawberries, sliced
- 1/4 cup granola (low sodium)
- 1 tablespoon honey (optional)
- 1 tablespoon chia seeds (optional)

Directions:

1. In serving glasses or bowls, layer 1/4 cup of Greek yogurt at the bottom.

2. Add a layer of sliced strawberries, followed by a sprinkle of granola and chia seeds.

3. Repeat the layering process with the remaining yogurt, strawberries, and granola.

4. Drizzle honey over the top if desired and serve immediately.

- **Nutritional Information per serving**: 200 calories,

- 14g protein, 28g carbohydrates, 5g total fat, 3g fiber,

- 10mg cholesterol, 80mg sodium, 300mg potassium,

- 15g sugars, 220 mg phosphorus.

CHAPTER 2:
LIGHT LUNCHES

14. Grilled Chicken and Apple Salad

Yield: 2 servings | **Prep time**: 10 minutes | **Cook time**: 10 minutes

Ingredients:

- 2 boneless, skinless chicken breasts and 1 small apple, thinly sliced
- 4 cups mixed greens (spinach, arugula, or lettuce)
- 1/4 cup of walnuts, chopped (unsalted) and 2 tablespoons of olive oil
- 1 tablespoon of balsamic vinegar and 1 teaspoon Dijon mustard and 1/4 teaspoon black pepper

Directions:

1. Season the chicken breasts with black pepper and grill over medium heat for 6-8 minutes on each side.

2. In a large bowl, toss the mixed greens with apple slices and walnuts. In a small bowl, whisk together the olive oil, balsamic vinegar, and mustard.

3. Top the salad with the grilled chicken slices and drizzle with the dressing. Serve immediately.

Nutritional Information per serving: 350 calories, 28g protein,

12g carbohydrates, 20g total fat, 4g fiber, 75mg cholesterol, 180mg sodium, 350mg potassium, 6g sugars,

280 mg phosphorus.

15. Tuna Salad with Cucumber and Dill

Yield: 2 servings | **Prep time**: 10 minutes | **Cook time**: 0 minutes

Ingredients:

- 1 can tuna in water (low-sodium, drained)
- 1/4 cup plain Greek yogurt
- 1/4 cup cucumber, diced
- 1 tablespoon fresh dill, chopped
- 1 tablespoon lemon juice
- 1/4 teaspoon black pepper
- 2 low-sodium whole wheat pita pockets (optional)

Directions:

1. In a medium bowl, mix the tuna, Greek yogurt, cucumber, dill, lemon juice, and black pepper until well combined.

2. Serve on its own or stuff into whole wheat pita pockets for a light lunch.

Nutritional Information per serving: 200 calories, 22g protein,

12g carbohydrates, 7g total fat, 1g fiber, 35mg cholesterol, 120mg sodium, 250mg potassium, 2g sugars,

215 mg phosphorus.

16. Roasted Vegetable Wraps

Yield: 2 servings | **Prep time**: 10 minutes | **Cook time**: 20 minutes

Ingredients:

- 1 small zucchini, sliced and 1 red bell pepper, sliced
- 1/2 red onion, sliced
- 1 tablespoon olive oil
- 1/4 teaspoon black pepper
- 2 low-sodium whole wheat wraps and 2 tablespoons hummus (low sodium)
- 1 cup fresh spinach leaves

Directions:

1. Preheat the oven to 400°F (200°C).

2. Toss the sliced zucchini, bell pepper, and onion with olive oil and black pepper. Spread the vegetables in a single layer on a baking sheet and roast for 15-20 minutes, or until tender.

3. Spread hummus evenly onto each wrap. Add the roasted vegetables and fresh spinach on top of the hummus and roll the wraps tightly.

4. Cut in half and serve warm or cold.

Nutritional Information per serving: 260 calories, 8g protein,

35g carbohydrates, 10g total fat, 6g fiber, 0mg cholesterol, 140mg sodium,

400mg potassium, 5g sugars,

145 mg phosphorus.

17. Chicken Salad with Cranberries and Pecans

Yield: 2 servings | **Prep time**: 10 minutes | **Cook time**: 0 minutes

Ingredients:

- 2 cups cooked, diced chicken breast (skinless)
- 1/4 cup plain Greek yogurt
- 1/4 cup dried cranberries (unsweetened)
- 1/4 cup chopped pecans (unsalted)
- 1/4 teaspoon black pepper
- 1 tablespoon lemon juice
- 2 cups mixed greens (optional, for serving)

Directions:

1. In a large bowl, combine the diced chicken, Greek yogurt, cranberries, pecans, black pepper, and lemon juice. Mix well.

2. Serve on its own or over a bed of mixed greens for a light and refreshing lunch.

Nutritional Information per serving: 320 calories, 30g protein,

14g carbohydrates, 16g total fat, 3g fiber, 80mg cholesterol, 100mg sodium, 320mg potassium, 8g sugars,

255 mg phosphorus.

18. Low-Sodium Turkey Lettuce Wraps

Yield: 2 servings | **Prep time**: 10 minutes | **Cook time**: 10 minutes

Ingredients:

- 1/2-pound ground turkey (lean, low-sodium) and 1 tablespoon olive oil
- 1/4 cup of diced onions and 1/4 cup diced bell peppers
- 1 teaspoon garlic powder and 1/4 teaspoon black pepper
- 6 large lettuce leaves (for wrapping)
- 1 tablespoon low-sodium soy sauce (optional) and 1/4 cup shredded carrots (for garnish)

Directions:

1. Heat olive oil in a skillet over medium heat. Add onions and bell peppers, sauté for 3-4 minutes until softened.
2. Add ground turkey, garlic powder, and black pepper. Cook for 5-7 minutes until the turkey is browned and fully cooked.
3. Spoon the turkey mixture into lettuce leaves and top with shredded carrots. Serve as wraps.

Nutritional Information per serving: 220 calories, 20g protein,

8g carbohydrates, 12g total fat, 2g fiber, 50mg cholesterol, 120mg sodium, 320mg potassium, 2g sugars,

240 mg phosphorus.

19. Renal-Friendly Caesar Salad

Yield: 2 servings | **Prep time**: 10 minutes | **Cook time**: 0 minutes

Ingredients:

- 4 cups romaine lettuce, chopped
- 1/4 cup grated Parmesan cheese (low sodium)
- 2 tablespoons of olive oil
- 1 tablespoon lemon juice and 1 teaspoon Dijon mustard
- 1/4 teaspoon black pepper
- 1 garlic clove, minced
- 1 slice low-sodium whole wheat bread, cubed (for croutons, optional)

Directions:

1. In a large bowl, toss the chopped romaine lettuce with grated Parmesan cheese.
2. In a small bowl, whisk together the olive oil, lemon juice, Dijon mustard, black pepper, and minced garlic to make the dressing.
3. Drizzle the dressing over the salad and toss it into the coat.

Nutritional Information per serving: 180 calories, 8g protein,

10g carbohydrates, 14g total fat, 3g fiber, 5mg cholesterol, 180mg sodium,

260mg potassium, 1g sugars, 1

60 mg phosphorus.

20. Stuffed Bell Peppers with Quinoa

Yield: 2 servings | **Prep time**: 10 minutes | **Cook time**: 30 minutes

Ingredients:

- 2 large bell peppers (any color), halved and seeds removed
- 1/2 cup cooked quinoa and 1/2 cup black beans
- 1/4 cup of diced tomatoes
- 1 tablespoon olive oil
- 1/4 teaspoon cumin and 1/4 teaspoon black pepper

Directions:

1. Preheat the oven to 375°F (190°C).
2. In a skillet, heat olive oil over medium heat. Add the diced tomatoes, black beans, quinoa, cumin, and black pepper. Cook for 5 minutes, stirring occasionally.
3. Fill each bell pepper in half with the quinoa mixture. Place the stuffed peppers in a baking dish.
4. Cover the dish with foil and bake for 20-25 minutes.
5. Serve warm and enjoy.

Nutritional Information per serving: 260 calories, 10g protein,

35g carbohydrates, 9g total fat, 8g fiber, 0mg cholesterol, 120mg sodium,

550mg potassium, 6g sugars,

240 mg phosphorus.

21. Zucchini Noodle Bowl with Grilled Salmon

Yield: 2 servings | **Prep time**: 10 minutes | **Cook time**: 10 minutes

Ingredients:

- 2 small zucchinis, spiralized into noodles and 2 salmon fillets (4 ounces each)
- 1 tablespoon olive oil (divided)
- 1 tablespoon lemon juice
- 1/4 teaspoon garlic powder
- 1/4 teaspoon black pepper

Directions:

1. Preheat the grill or a grill pan over medium-high heat. Brush the salmon fillets with 1/2 tablespoon olive oil, lemon juice, garlic powder, and black pepper.
2. Grill the salmon for 4-5 minutes on each side, or until fully cooked and flaky.
3. In a skillet, heat the remaining olive oil over medium heat. Add the spiralized zucchini noodles and sauté for 2-3 minutes until tender but still firm.
4. Serve the salmon on top of the zucchini noodles and garnish with fresh parsley.

Nutritional Information per serving: 300 calories, 28g protein,

6g carbohydrates, 18g total fat, 2g fiber, 70mg cholesterol, 100mg sodium, 500mg potassium, 1g sugars,

380 mg phosphorus.

22. Kidney-Friendly Lentil Soup

Yield: 4 servings | **Prep time**: 10 minutes | **Cook time**: 30 minutes

Ingredients:

- 1/2 cup dried lentils, rinsed
- 4 cups of water
- 1/2 cup diced carrots
- 1/2 cup diced celery
- 1/4 cup diced onions
- 1 tablespoon olive oil
- 1/4 teaspoon cumin
- 1/4 teaspoon black pepper, 1 bay leaf

Directions:

1. In a large pot, heat olive oil over medium heat. Add the onions, carrots, and celery, and sauté for 5 minutes until softened.

2. Add the rinsed lentils, water, cumin, black pepper, and bay leaf to the pot. Bring to a boil, then reduce heat and simmer for 25-30 minutes, or until the lentils are tender.

3. Remove the bay leaves before serving and enjoy the warm soup.

Nutritional Information per serving: 180 calories, 10g protein,

30g carbohydrates, 4g total fat, 8g fiber, 0mg cholesterol, 60mg sodium,

350mg potassium, 4g sugars,

180 mg phosphorus.

23. Mediterranean Couscous Salad

Yield: 2 servings | **Prep time**: 10 minutes | **Cook time**: 10 minutes

Ingredients:

- 1/2 cup couscous (uncooked)
- 1/2 cup of water
- 1/4 cup diced cucumber
- 1/4 cup of diced cherry tomatoes
- 1/4 cup chopped parsley
- 1 tablespoon olive oil
- 1 tablespoon lemon juice
- 1/4 teaspoon black pepper
- 1 tablespoon of feta cheese

Directions:

1. Bring water to boil in a small pot. Stir in couscous, cover, and remove from heat. Let it sit for 5 minutes, then fluff with a fork.

2. In a large bowl, combine the cooked couscous with cucumber, cherry tomatoes, parsley, olive oil, lemon juice, and black pepper. Toss well.

3. If desired, sprinkle with feta cheese before serving.

Nutritional Information per serving: 200 calories, 5g protein,

30g carbohydrates, 8g total fat, 3g fiber, 0mg cholesterol, 70mg sodium,

200mg potassium, 2g sugars,

120 mg phosphorus.

24. Renal-Friendly Egg Salad Sandwich

Yield: 2 servings | **Prep time**: 10 minutes | **Cook time**: 0 minutes

Ingredients:

- 4 large egg whites, hard-boiled and chopped
- 1/4 cup plain Greek yogurt
- 1 tablespoon mustard
- 1 tablespoon chopped chives
- 1/4 teaspoon black pepper
- 2 slices of low-sodium whole wheat bread
- 1 lettuce leaf (optional)

Directions:

1. In a bowl, mix the chopped egg whites, Greek yogurt, mustard, chives, and black pepper until well combined.
2. Spread the egg salad mixture onto the bread slices. Add lettuce, if desired.
3. Serve as an open-faced sandwich or a traditional sandwich with both slices of bread.

Nutritional Information per serving: 180 calories, 14g protein,

22g carbohydrates, 5g total fat, 2g fiber, 0mg cholesterol, 130mg sodium,

150mg potassium, 3g sugars,

120 mg phosphorus.

25. Low-Sodium Grilled Chicken Tacos

Yield: 2 servings | **Prep time**: 10 minutes | **Cook time**: 10 minutes

Ingredients:

- 2 boneless, skinless chicken breasts. 1 tablespoon olive oil and 1 tablespoon lemon juice
- 1/4 teaspoon garlic powder, 1/4 teaspoon cumin and 1/4 teaspoon black pepper
- 4 small low-sodium corn tortillas
- 1/4 cup shredded lettuce and 1/4 cup of diced tomatoes

Directions:

1. Preheat a grill or grill pan over medium heat. Coat the chicken breasts with olive oil, lemon juice, garlic powder, cumin, and black pepper.
2. Grill the chicken for 5-6 minutes on each side, or until fully cooked. Let it rest for 5 minutes, then slice it into strips. Warm the tortillas on the grill for about 30 seconds on each side.
3. Assemble the tacos by adding chicken, shredded lettuce, diced tomatoes, and avocado.

Nutritional Information per serving: 300 calories, 25g protein,

20g carbohydrates, 12g total fat, 4g fiber, 65mg cholesterol, 120mg sodium, 350mg potassium, 2g sugars,

240 mg phosphorus.

26. Roasted Butternut Squash Soup

Yield: 4 servings | **Prep time**: 10 minutes | **Cook time**: 40 minutes

Ingredients:

- 1 medium butternut squash, peeled and cubed
- 1 tablespoon olive oil
- 1/2 teaspoon ground cinnamon
- 1/4 teaspoon black pepper
- 4 cups low-sodium vegetable broth
- 1 small onion, diced
- 2 cloves garlic, minced
- 1/2 cup almond milk (unsweetened)

Directions:

1. Preheat the oven to 400°F (200°C). Toss the cubed butternut squash with olive oil, cinnamon, and black pepper. Spread on a baking sheet and roast for 25-30 minutes, or until tender.

2. In a large pot, sauté the diced onion and minced garlic in a bit of olive oil until softened, about 5 minutes.

3. Add the roasted butternut squash and vegetable broth to the pot. Bring to a boil, then reduce heat and simmer for 10 minutes.

4. Using an immersion blender, blend the soup until smooth. Stir in almond milk and heat through.

5. Serve warm, garnished with a sprinkle of cinnamon if desired.

Nutritional Information per serving: 160 calories, 4g protein,

30g carbohydrates, 5g total fat, 5g fiber, 0mg cholesterol, 70mg sodium,

400mg potassium, 5g sugars,

120 mg phosphorus.

Chapter 3:

Heartier Dinners

27. Baked Lemon Herb Tilapia

Yield: 2 servings | **Prep time**: 5 minutes | **Cook time**: 15 minutes

Ingredients:

- 2 tilapia fillets
- 1 tablespoon olive oil
- 1 tablespoon lemon juice
- 1 teaspoon dried oregano
- 1/4 teaspoon black pepper
- 1 tablespoon fresh parsley, chopped (optional)

Directions:

1. Preheat the oven to 375°F (190°C). Line a baking sheet with parchment paper or lightly grease it with olive oil.

2. In a small bowl, mix the olive oil, lemon juice, oregano, and black pepper. Brush the mixture evenly over both sides of the tilapia fillets.

3. Place the fillets on the baking sheet and bake for 12-15 minutes, or until the fish is flaky and fully cooked.

4. Garnish with fresh parsley and serve with roasted vegetables or a light salad.

Nutritional Information per serving: 200 calories, 25g protein,

1g carbohydrates, 10g total fat, 1g fiber, 55mg cholesterol, 120mg sodium, 450mg potassium, 0g sugars,

240 mg phosphorus.

28. Grilled Chicken Breast with Herb Sauce

Yield: 2 servings | **Prep time**: 10 minutes | **Cook time**: 10 minutes

Ingredients:

- 2 boneless, skinless chicken breasts
- 1 tablespoon olive oil, 1 tablespoon lemon juice, 1 teaspoon dried thyme and 1 teaspoon dried oregano
- 1/4 teaspoon garlic powder and 1/4 teaspoon black pepper

Directions:

1. Preheat the grill or a grill pan over medium heat.

2. In a small bowl, mix the olive oil, lemon juice, thyme, oregano, garlic powder, and black pepper.

3. Coat the chicken breasts with herb sauce.

4. Grill the chicken for 5-6 minutes on each side, or until fully cooked and the internal temperature reaches 165°F (75°C).

5. Garnish with fresh parsley before serving. Serve with a side of steamed vegetables.

Nutritional Information per serving: 280 calories, 28g protein,

0g carbohydrates, 18g total fat, 0g fiber, 85mg cholesterol, 120mg sodium, 350mg potassium, 0g sugars,

230 mg phosphorus.

29. Low-Sodium Beef Stir-Fry

Yield: 2 servings | **Prep time**: 10 minutes | **Cook time**: 10 minutes

Ingredients:

- 1/2-pound lean beef (sliced thin)
- 1 tablespoon olive oil
- 1/4 cup low-sodium soy sauce
- 1/2 cup broccoli florets and 1/2 red bell pepper, sliced
- 1/4 cup carrots, sliced
- 1 tablespoon fresh ginger, minced
- 1 garlic clove, minced

Directions:

1. Heat olive oil in a large skillet or wok over medium-high heat. Add the beef strips and stir-fry for 2-3 minutes until browned. Remove from the skillet and set aside.

2. In the same skillet, add the garlic and ginger, followed by the broccoli, bell pepper, and carrots. Stir-fry for 4-5 minutes.

3. Return the beef to the skillet and add the low-sodium soy sauce. Cook for 2 more minutes, stirring to combine. Serve warm with steamed rice.

Nutritional Information per serving: 300 calories, 25g protein,

12g carbohydrates, 15g total fat, 4g fiber, 60mg cholesterol, 150mg sodium, 450mg potassium, 4g sugars,

260 mg phosphorus.

30. Baked Salmon with Dill and Lemon

Yield: 2 servings | **Prep time**: 5 minutes | **Cook time**: 15 minutes

Ingredients:

- 2 salmon fillets (4 ounces each)
- 1 tablespoon olive oil
- 1 tablespoon lemon juice
- 1 teaspoon dried dill
- 1/4 teaspoon garlic powder
- 1/4 teaspoon black pepper

Directions:

1. Preheat the oven to 375°F (190°C). Line a baking sheet with parchment paper or lightly grease it with olive oil.

2. In a small bowl, mix the olive oil, lemon juice, dried dill, garlic powder, and black pepper.

3. Brush the salmon fillets with the mixture on both sides.

4. Place the fillets on the baking sheet and bake for 12-15 minutes, or until the salmon is fully cooked and flakes easily with a fork.

5. Garnish with fresh dill before serving. Serve with a side of roasted vegetables or quinoa.

Nutritional Information per serving: 290 calories, 26g protein,

1g carbohydrates, 18g total fat, 1g fiber, 70mg cholesterol, 100mg sodium, 500mg potassium, 0g sugars,

320 mg phosphorus.

31. Garlic-Roasted Pork Tenderloin

Yield: 4 servings | **Prep time**: 10 minutes | **Cook time**: 25 minutes

Ingredients:

- 1 pound pork tenderloin
- 2 tablespoons of olive oil
- 3 garlic cloves, minced
- 1 tablespoon fresh rosemary, chopped
- 1 tablespoon lemon juice
- 1/4 teaspoon black pepper
- 1/4 teaspoon garlic powder

Directions:

1. Preheat the oven to 400°F. In a small bowl, mix the olive oil, minced garlic, rosemary, lemon juice, black pepper, and garlic powder.

2. Rub the garlic-herb mixture all over the pork tenderloin. Place the pork tenderloin in a roasting pan and bake for 25-30 minutes, or until the internal temperature reaches 145°F

3. Let the pork rest for 5 minutes before slicing. Serve with roasted vegetables or mashed potatoes.

Nutritional Information per serving: 270 calories, 24g protein,

0g carbohydrates, 18g total fat, 0g fiber, 80mg cholesterol, 70mg sodium,

450mg potassium, 0g sugars,

240 mg phosphorus

32. Chicken and Rice Casserole

Yield: 4 servings | **Prep time**: 10 minutes | **Cook time**: 30 minutes

Ingredients:

- 2 boneless, skinless chicken breasts, cubed. 1 cup cooked white rice, 1 tablespoon olive oil
- 1/2 cup low-sodium chicken broth, 1/2 cup plain Greek yogurt, 1/2 cup low-fat shredded cheddar cheese, 1/2 cup broccoli florets
- 1/4 teaspoon black pepper and 1/4 teaspoon garlic powder

Directions:

1. Preheat the oven to 375°F. Grease a baking dish with olive oil.

2. Heat the olive oil over medium heat and sauté the chicken cubes until browned, for about 5-7 minutes.

3. In a large bowl, combine the cooked rice, chicken, chicken broth, Greek yogurt, shredded cheese, broccoli, black pepper, and garlic powder.

4. Transfer the mixture to the prepared baking dish and bake for 20-25 minutes, Serve warm.

Nutritional Information per serving: 350 calories, 28g protein,

30g carbohydrates, 12g total fat, 2g fiber, 80mg cholesterol, 150mg sodium, 350mg potassium, 4g sugars,

280 mg phosphorus

33. Stuffed Zucchini Boats with Ground Turkey

Yield: 2 servings | Prep time: 10 minutes | Cook time: 20 minutes

Ingredients:

- 2 medium zucchinis
- 1/2-pound ground turkey
- 1/4 cup of diced onions, 1/4 cup of diced tomatoes
- 1/4 teaspoon garlic powder, 1/4 teaspoon black pepper
- 1 tablespoon olive oil

Directions:

1. Preheat the oven to 375°F. Slice the zucchini half lengthwise and scoop out the seeds to create boats. Set aside.

2. Heat olive oil in a skillet over medium heat. Add onions and cook for 3-4 minutes. Add ground turkey, garlic powder, and black pepper, and cook until the turkey is browned, about 6-8 minutes.

3. Stir in the diced tomatoes and cook for another 2 minutes. Spoon the turkey mixture.

4. Bake for 15-20 minutes, or until the zucchini is tender and the cheese is melted.

Nutritional Information per serving: 240 calories, 25g protein,

8g carbohydrates, 12g total fat, 3g fiber, 60mg cholesterol, 120mg sodium, 500mg potassium, 4g sugars,

270 mg phosphorus.

34. Low-Sodium Beef Chili

Yield: 4 servings | Prep time: 10 minutes | Cook time: 40 minutes

Ingredients:

- 1/2-pound lean ground beef, 1/2 cup diced onions, 1/2 cup diced bell peppers
- 1 can (15 ounces) low sodium diced tomatoes, 1 can (15 ounces) kidney beans
- 1 tablespoon olive oil, 1 tablespoon chili powder
- 1 teaspoon cumin
- 1/4 teaspoon black pepper, 1/4 teaspoon garlic powder

Directions:

1. Heat olive oil in a large pot over medium heat. Add onions and bell peppers, and sauté for 3-4 minutes until softened.

2. Add the ground beef and cook until browned, for about 6-8 minutes. Drain any excess fat.

3. Stir in the diced tomatoes, kidney beans, chili powder, cumin, black pepper, and garlic powder.

4. Bring to a boil, then reduce heat to a simmer. Cover and cook for 30 minutes, stirring occasionally.

Nutritional Information per serving: 270 calories, 24g protein,

30g carbohydrates, 8g total fat, 8g fiber, 50mg cholesterol, 140mg sodium, 600mg potassium, 6g sugars,

300 mg phosphorus.

35. Herb-Crusted Baked Cod

Yield: 2 servings | **Prep time**: 10 minutes | **Cook time**: 15 minutes

Ingredients:

- 2 cod fillets (4 ounces each)
- 1 tablespoon olive oil, 1/4 cup of breadcrumbs
- 1 tablespoon fresh parsley, chopped, 1 teaspoon dried thyme, 1 teaspoon dried oregano
- 1/4 teaspoon black pepper, 1 tablespoon lemon juice

Directions:

1. Preheat the oven to 375°F. Line a baking sheet with parchment paper or lightly grease it with olive oil.
2. In a small bowl, mix the breadcrumbs, parsley, thyme, oregano, black pepper, and lemon juice.
3. Brush the cod fillets with olive oil and press the herb mixture evenly onto the fillets.
4. Place the cod on the baking sheet and bake for 12-15 minutes, or until the fish is flaky and cooked.
5. Serve warm.

Nutritional Information per serving: 220 calories, 25g protein,

10g carbohydrates, 10g total fat, 1g fiber, 60mg cholesterol, 120mg sodium, 450mg potassium, 0g sugars,

300 mg phosphorus

36. Roasted Turkey with Cranberry Relish

Yield: 4 servings | **Prep time**: 15 minutes | **Cook time**: 1 hour 30 minutes

Ingredients:

- 1 small turkey breast, 2 tablespoons of olive oil
- 1 tablespoon fresh rosemary, chopped, 1 tablespoon fresh thyme, chopped
- 1/4 teaspoon black pepper, 1/4 cup low-sodium chicken broth

For the Cranberry Relish:

- 1 cup fresh cranberries, 1 tablespoon honey, 1/4 cup of water, 1/2 teaspoon orange zest

Directions:

1. Preheat the oven to 350°F. Rub the turkey breast with olive oil, rosemary, thyme, and black pepper.
2. Place the turkey breast in a roasting pan and pour the chicken broth into the bottom of the pan.
3. Roast for 1 hour 30 minutes. Prepare the cranberry relish by simmering cranberries, water, honey, and orange zest in a saucepan for 10-15 minutes.

Nutritional Information per serving: 320 calories, 35g protein,

12g carbohydrates, 12g total fat, 1g fiber, 80mg cholesterol, 140mg sodium, 350mg potassium, 8g sugars,

270 mg phosphorus

37. Spaghetti Squash with Tomato Sauce

Yield: 2 servings | **Prep time**: 10 minutes | **Cook time**: 40 minutes

Ingredients:

- 1 medium spaghetti squash, 1 tablespoon olive oil
- 1/2 cup low-sodium tomato sauce, 1/4 cup of diced tomatoes
- 1 clove garlic, minced, 1/2 teaspoon dried basil, 1/4 teaspoon black pepper

Directions:

1. Preheat the oven to 400°F. Cut the spaghetti squash half lengthwise and remove the seeds. Brush the inside with olive oil and place cut side down on a baking sheet.

2. Roast for 30-40 minutes, or until the flesh is tender and can be scraped into strands with a fork.

3. While the squash is roasting, heat the tomato sauce, diced tomatoes, garlic, basil, and black pepper in a saucepan over medium heat. Simmer for 10 minutes. Scrape the flesh of the spaghetti squash into strands and divide between two plates.

Nutritional Information per serving: 180 calories, 4g protein,

30g carbohydrates, 7g total fat, 6g fiber, 0mg cholesterol, 50mg sodium,

500mg potassium, 7g sugars,

120 mg phosphorus.

38. Grilled Shrimp with Garlic Butter

Yield: 2 servings | **Prep time**: 10 minutes | **Cook time**: 5 minutes

Ingredients:

- 12 large shrimp, peeled and deveined
- 2 tablespoons of olive oil
- 2 tablespoons unsalted butter
- 2 garlic cloves, minced
- 1 tablespoon lemon juice
- 1/4 teaspoon black pepper

Directions:

1. Preheat a grill or grill pan to medium-high heat.

2. In a small skillet, melt the butter and olive oil over medium heat. Add the minced garlic and sauté for 1-2 minutes until fragrant.

3. Toss the shrimp in the garlic butter mixture, coating them well. Grill the shrimp for 2-3 minutes on each side until they are pink and fully cooked.

4. Remove from the grill, drizzle lemon juice, and sprinkle with black pepper and fresh parsley.

Nutritional Information per serving: 210 calories, 20g protein,

2g carbohydrates, 14g total fat, 0g fiber, 190mg cholesterol, 90mg sodium, 250mg potassium, 0g sugars,

230 mg phosphorus.

39. Renal-Friendly Meatloaf

Yield: 4 servings | **Prep time**: 10 minutes | **Cook time**: 45 minutes

Ingredients:

- 1/2-pound lean ground beef
- 1/2-pound ground turkey (lean)
- 1/4 cup plain breadcrumbs (low sodium)
- 1/4 cup plain Greek yogurt
- 1 small onion, finely chopped
- 1 garlic clove, minced
- 1/4 teaspoon black pepper
- 1 tablespoon fresh parsley, chopped
- 1 egg white, lightly beaten
- 1/4 cup low-sodium ketchup (optional, for topping)

Directions:

1. Preheat the oven to 375°F (190°C).

2. In a large bowl, mix the ground beef, ground turkey, breadcrumbs, Greek yogurt, onion, garlic, black pepper, parsley, and egg white until well combined.

3. Transfer the mixture to a loaf pan and press it down evenly.

4. Optionally, spread the low-sodium ketchup on top of the meatloaf for added flavor.

5. Bake for 40-45 minutes, or until the internal temperature reaches 165°F (75°C).

6. Let the meatloaf rest for 5 minutes before slicing and serving.

Nutritional Information per serving: 290 calories, 30g protein,

12g carbohydrates, 14g total fat, 1g fiber, 90mg cholesterol, 130mg sodium, 450mg potassium, 3g sugars,

270 mg phosphorus

Chapter 4:

Snacks and Sides

40. Baked Sweet Potato Chips

Yield: 2 servings | **Prep time**: 5 minutes | **Cook time**: 20 minutes

Ingredients:

- 1 large, sweet potato
- 1 tablespoon olive oil
- 1/4 teaspoon black pepper
- 1/4 teaspoon paprika

Directions:

1. Preheat the oven to 400°F (200°C). Line a baking sheet with parchment paper.

2. Thinly slice the sweet potato into rounds, about 1/8 inch thick.

3. In a bowl, toss the sweet potato slices with olive oil, black pepper, and paprika until evenly coated.

4. Spread the slices in a single layer on the prepared baking sheet.

5. Bake for 15-20 minutes, flipping halfway through, until crispy and golden brown.

6. Serve as a snack or side dish.

Nutritional Information per serving: 160 calories, 2g protein,

24g carbohydrates, 7g total fat, 4g fiber, 0mg cholesterol, 20mg sodium,

400mg potassium, 4g sugars,

60 mg phosphorus.

41. Hummus with Cucumber Slices

Yield: 2 servings | **Prep time**: 5 minutes | **Cook time**: 0 minutes

Ingredients:

- 1/2 cup canned chickpeas (rinsed, low sodium)
- 1 tablespoon tahini
- 1 tablespoon olive oil
- 1 tablespoon lemon juice
- 1/4 teaspoon garlic powder
- 1/4 teaspoon black pepper
- 1/2 cucumber, sliced

Directions:

1. In a food processor, blend the chickpeas, tahini, olive oil, lemon juice, garlic powder, and black pepper until smooth. If the hummus is too thick, add a little water to reach your desired consistency.

2. Serve the hummus with cucumber slices for dipping.

Nutritional Information per serving: 180 calories, 5g protein,

16g carbohydrates, 10g total fat, 5g fiber, 0mg cholesterol, 80mg sodium,

200mg potassium, 1g sugars,

110 mg phosphorus

42. Low-Sodium Guacamole with Bell Pepper Sticks

Yield: 2 servings | **Prep time**: 5 minutes | **Cook time**: 0 minutes

Ingredients:

- 1 ripe avocado
- 1 tablespoon lime juice
- 1/4 teaspoon garlic powder
- 1/4 teaspoon black pepper
- 1 tablespoon fresh cilantro, chopped
- 1 small red bell pepper, sliced into sticks

Directions:

1. In a bowl, mash the avocado with lime juice, garlic powder, black pepper, and cilantro until smooth.

2. Serve the guacamole with bell pepper sticks for dipping.

Nutritional Information per serving: 160 calories, 2g protein,

12g carbohydrates, 12g total fat, 7g fiber, 0mg cholesterol, 10mg sodium,

400mg potassium, 2g sugars,

60 mg phosphorus

43. Quinoa Salad with Apples and Walnuts

Yield: 2 servings | **Prep time**: 10 minutes | **Cook time**: 15 minutes

Ingredients:

- 1/2 cup quinoa, rinsed
- 1 cup of water
- 1 small apple, diced
- 1/4 cup of walnuts, chopped (unsalted)
- 1 tablespoon olive oil
- 1 tablespoon lemon juice
- 1/4 teaspoon black pepper
- 1 tablespoon fresh parsley, chopped (optional)

Directions:

1. In a small pot, bring water to a boil. Add quinoa, reduce heat, and simmer for 12-15 minutes, or until the water is absorbed and the quinoa is tender. Fluff with a fork and let it cool slightly.

2. In a large bowl, combine the cooked quinoa, diced apple, chopped walnuts, olive oil, lemon juice, black pepper, and parsley. Toss well.

Nutritional Information per serving: 250 calories, 7g protein,

30g carbohydrates, 12g total fat, 4g fiber, 0mg cholesterol, 10mg sodium,

250mg potassium, 8g sugars,

180 mg phosphorus.

44. Grilled Vegetable Skewers

Yield: 2 servings | **Prep time**: 10 minutes | **Cook time**: 10 minutes

Ingredients:

- 1 small zucchini, sliced
- 1 red bell pepper, cut into chunks
- 1 yellow bell pepper, cut into chunks
- 1/2 red onion, cut into chunks
- 1 tablespoon olive oil
- 1 tablespoon of balsamic vinegar
- 1/4 teaspoon black pepper, 1/4 teaspoon garlic powder

Directions:

1. Preheat the grill to medium heat.

2. In a bowl, toss the zucchini, bell peppers, and onion with olive oil, balsamic vinegar, black pepper, and garlic powder until well coated.

3. Thread the vegetables onto skewers.

4. Grill the vegetable skewers for 8-10 minutes, turning occasionally, until the vegetables are tender and slightly charred.

Nutritional Information per serving: 150 calories, 2g protein,

12g carbohydrates, 10g total fat, 3g fiber, 0mg cholesterol, 10mg sodium,

250mg potassium, 6g sugars,

60 mg phosphorus

45. Zucchini Fritters

Yield: 2 servings | **Prep time**: 10 minutes | **Cook time**: 10 minutes

Ingredients:

- 1 medium zucchini, grated
- 1/4 cup of all-purpose flour
- 1 large egg white
- 1 tablespoon olive oil
- 1/4 teaspoon garlic powder
- 1/4 teaspoon black pepper
- 1 tablespoon fresh parsley, chopped (optional)

Directions:

1. Place the grated zucchini in a clean kitchen towel and squeeze out excess moisture.

2. In a bowl, mix the zucchini, flour, egg white, garlic powder, black pepper, and parsley.

3. Heat olive oil in a non-stick skillet over medium heat. Drop spoonsful of the zucchini mixture into the skillet and flatten them slightly with a spatula.

4. Cook for 3-4 minutes on each side, or until golden brown and crispy.

Nutritional Information per serving: 180 calories, 5g protein,

16g carbohydrates, 10g total fat, 2g fiber, 0mg cholesterol, 90mg sodium,

250mg potassium, 3g sugars,

120 mg phosphorus.

46. Roasted Carrots and Parsnips

Yield: 2 servings | **Prep time**: 5 minutes | **Cook time**: 25 minutes

Ingredients:

- 2 medium carrots, peeled and cut into sticks
- 2 medium parsnips, peeled and cut into sticks
- 1 tablespoon olive oil
- 1/4 teaspoon black pepper
- 1/4 teaspoon dried thyme

Directions:

1. Preheat the oven to 400°F (200°C). Line a baking sheet with parchment paper.
2. In a large bowl, toss the carrots and parsnips with olive oil, black pepper, and thyme.
3. Spread the vegetables in a single layer on the baking sheet.
4. Roast for 20-25 minutes, or until the vegetables are tender and slightly caramelized, stirring halfway through.
5. Serve warm as a side dish.

Nutritional Information per serving: 150 calories, 2g protein,

20g carbohydrates, 7g total fat, 5g fiber, 0mg cholesterol, 20mg sodium,

500mg potassium, 5g sugars,

80 mg phosphorus

47. Rice Cakes with Peanut Butter

Yield: 2 servings | **Prep time**: 5 minutes | **Cook time**: 0 minutes

Ingredients:

- 2 unsalted rice cakes
- 2 tablespoons of natural peanut butter (unsweetened)
- 1/4 cup sliced banana (optional)

Directions:

1. Spread 1 tablespoon of peanut butter on each rice cake.
2. Top with sliced bananas if desired.
3. Serve as a snack or light breakfast option.

Nutritional Information per serving: 180 calories, 6g protein,

16g carbohydrates, 12g total fat, 2g fiber, 0mg cholesterol, 10mg sodium,

150mg potassium, 3g sugars,

130 mg phosphorus

48. Popcorn with Garlic and Herb Seasoning

Yield: 2 servings | **Prep time**: 5 minutes | **Cook time**: 5 minutes

Ingredients:

- 1/4 cup popcorn kernels
- 1 tablespoon olive oil
- 1/4 teaspoon garlic powder
- 1/4 teaspoon dried oregano
- 1/4 teaspoon dried thyme
- 1/4 teaspoon black pepper

Directions:

1. Heat the olive oil in a large pot over medium heat. Add the popcorn kernels and cover with a lid.

2. Shake the pot occasionally to prevent burning. Once the popping slows down, remove from heat.

3. Transfer the popcorn to a large bowl and sprinkle with garlic powder, oregano, thyme, and black pepper. Toss well to coat.

4. Serve immediately as a healthy snack.

Nutritional Information per serving: 100 calories, 2g protein,

12g carbohydrates, 5g total fat, 2g fiber, 0mg cholesterol, 5mg sodium,

90mg potassium, 0g sugars,

50 mg phosphorus.

49. Kidney-Friendly Deviled Eggs

Yield: 4 servings (8 halves) | **Prep time**: 10 minutes | **Cook time**: 10 minutes

Ingredients:

- 4 large eggs
- 1/4 cup plain Greek yogurt
- 1/2 teaspoon Dijon mustard
- 1/4 teaspoon garlic powder
- 1/4 teaspoon black pepper
- 1 tablespoon fresh chives, chopped (optional, for garnish)

Directions:

1. Place the eggs in a saucepan and cover with water. Bring to a boil, then remove from heat and cover. Let's sit for 10 minutes.

2. Drain the eggs and place them in cold water to cool. Once cooled, peel the eggs and slice them half lengthwise.

3. Remove the yolks and place them in a bowl. Mash with Greek yogurt, Dijon mustard, garlic powder, and black pepper until smooth.

4. Spoon the mixture back into the egg whites. Garnish with chopped chives if desired.

Nutritional Information per serving: 100 calories, 7g protein,

3g carbohydrates, 6g total fat, 0g fiber, 10mg cholesterol, 60mg sodium,

70mg potassium, 1g sugars,

110 mg phosphorus.

50. Low-Sodium Potato Salad

Yield: 4 servings | **Prep time**: 10 minutes | **Cook time**: 15 minutes

Ingredients:

- 4 small red potatoes, diced
- 1/4 cup plain Greek yogurt
- 1 tablespoon Dijon mustard
- 1 tablespoon lemon juice
- 1/4 cup celery, finely chopped
- 1 tablespoon fresh dill, chopped
- 1/4 teaspoon black pepper

Directions:

1. Place the diced potatoes in a pot and cover with water. Bring to a boil and cook for 10-15 minutes until tender. Drain and let cool.

2. In a large bowl, mix the Greek yogurt, Dijon mustard, lemon juice, celery, dill, and black pepper.

3. Add the cooled potatoes to the bowl and toss gently to combine.

4. Serve chilled or at room temperature.

Nutritional Information per serving: 120 calories, 4g protein,

22g carbohydrates, 2g total fat, 3g fiber, 0mg cholesterol, 20mg sodium,

400mg potassium, 2g sugars,

120 mg phosphorus.

51. Mango and Cucumber Salsa

Yield: 2 servings | **Prep time**: 10 minutes | **Cook time**: 0 minutes

Ingredients:

- 1/2 ripe mango, diced
- 1/2 cucumber, diced
- 1 tablespoon lime juice
- 1 tablespoon fresh cilantro, chopped
- 1/4 teaspoon black pepper
- 1/4 teaspoon garlic powder

Directions:

1. In a bowl, combine the diced mango, cucumber, lime juice, cilantro, black pepper, and garlic powder.

2. Toss well mixed.

3. Serve immediately with baked tortilla chips or as a side dish with grilled fish or chicken.

Nutritional Information per serving:

60 calories, 1g protein,

15g carbohydrates, 0g total fat, 2g fiber, 0mg cholesterol, 5mg sodium,

150mg potassium, 10g sugars,

20 mg phosphorus.

52. Fresh Apple Slices with Almond Butter

Yield: 2 servings | **Prep time**: 5 minutes | **Cook time**: 0 minutes

Ingredients:

- 1 medium apple, sliced
- 2 tablespoons almond butter (unsweetened)

Directions:

.

1. Slice the apple into wedges.
2. Serve with almond butter for dipping.

Nutritional Information per serving: 180 calories, 4g protein,

20g carbohydrates, 9g total fat, 4g fiber, 0mg cholesterol, 5mg sodium,

200mg potassium, 12g sugars,

90 mg phosphorus.

Chapter 5:

Soup and Stews

53. Low-Sodium Chicken Noodle Soup

Yield: 4 servings | **Prep time**: 10 minutes | **Cook time**: 30 minutes

Ingredients:

- 1 boneless, skinless chicken breast, 4 cups low-sodium chicken broth
- 1/2 cup of carrots, diced, 1/2 cup of celery, diced
- 1/4 cup of onions, diced, 1/2 cup of whole wheat noodles, 1 tablespoon olive oil, 1/4 teaspoon black pepper, 1/4 teaspoon dried thyme, 1 bay leaf

Directions:

1. In a large pot, heat olive oil over medium heat. Sauté onions, carrots, and celery until softened, about 5 minutes.
2. Add chicken breast, low-sodium broth, black pepper, thyme, and bay leaf. Bring to a boil, then reduce heat to a simmer. Cook for 15 minutes.
3. Remove the chicken breast, shred it with two forks, and return it to the pot. Add the whole wheat noodles and simmer for another 8-10 minutes.

Nutritional Information per serving: 180 calories, 15g protein,

18g carbohydrates, 6g total fat, 2g fiber, 40mg cholesterol, 140mg sodium, 350mg potassium, 4g sugars,

150 mg phosphorus

54. Carrot and Ginger Soup

Yield: 4 servings | **Prep time**: 10 minutes | **Cook time**: 20 minutes

Ingredients:

- 4 large carrots, peeled and chopped
- 1 small onion, chopped, 1 tablespoon olive oil.
- 1 tablespoon fresh ginger, minced
- 4 cups low-sodium vegetable broth
- 1/4 teaspoon black pepper, 1/4 teaspoon ground cumin

Directions:

1. Heat olive oil in a large pot over medium heat. Add onions and ginger and sauté for 5 minutes until softened.
2. Add the chopped carrots and sauté for another 5 minutes. Pour in the low-sodium vegetable broth, black pepper, and cumin. Bring to a boil, then reduce to a simmer and cook for 15-20 minutes until the carrots are tender.
3. Using an immersion blender or regular blender, puree the soup until smooth.

Nutritional Information per serving: 120 calories, 2g protein,

20g carbohydrates, 4g total fat, 4g fiber, 0mg cholesterol, 70mg sodium,

400mg potassium, 6g sugars,

70 mg phosphorus.

55. Creamy Cauliflower Soup

Yield: 4 servings | **Prep time**: 10 minutes | **Cook time**: 20 minutes

Ingredients:

- 1 medium head of cauliflower, chopped, 1 small onion, diced, 2 cloves garlic, minced, 1 tablespoon olive oil

- 4 cups low-sodium vegetable broth, 1/2 cup unsweetened almond milk

- 1/4 teaspoon black pepper, 1/4 teaspoon ground nutmeg

Directions:

1. Heat olive oil in a large pot over medium heat. Add onions and garlic and sauté for 5 minutes until softened.

2. Add the chopped cauliflower, vegetable broth, black pepper, and nutmeg. Bring to boil, then reduce heat to a simmer and cook for 15-20 minutes until the cauliflower is tender.

3. Using an immersion blender, puree the soup until smooth., Stir in the almond milk and heat through for another 2-3 minutes.

Nutritional Information per serving: 130 calories, 3g protein,

15g carbohydrates, 6g total fat, 4g fiber, 0mg cholesterol, 60mg sodium,

400mg potassium, 4g sugars,

80 mg phosphorus.

56. Chicken and Barley Stew

Yield: 4 servings | **Prep time**: 10 minutes | **Cook time**: 45 minutes

Ingredients:

- 1 boneless, skinless chicken breast, cubed

- 1/2 cup pearl barley, rinsed

- 4 cups low-sodium chicken broth

- 1/2 cup of carrots, diced, 1/2 cup of celery, diced, 1/2 cup of onions, diced

- 1 tablespoon olive oil

- 1/4 teaspoon black pepper, 1/4 teaspoon dried thyme, 1 bay leaf

Directions:

1. In a large pot, heat olive oil over medium heat. Sauté onions, carrots, and celery until softened, about 5 minutes.

2. Add the cubed chicken and cook for another 5 minutes until browned.

3. Stir in the barley, chicken broth, black pepper, thyme, and bay leaf. Bring to a boil, then reduce heat and simmer for 30-40 minutes, or until the barley is tender. Remove the bay leaves and serve warm.

Nutritional Information per serving: 250 calories, 20g protein,

30g carbohydrates, 6g total fat, 5g fiber, 40mg cholesterol, 140mg sodium, 500mg potassium, 4g sugars,

180 mg phosphorus

57. Beef and Vegetable Stew

Yield: 4 servings | **Prep time**: 10 minutes | **Cook time**: 1 hour

Ingredients:

- 1/2-pound lean beef, cubed, 2 cups of low-sodium beef broth
- 1/2 cup carrots, sliced, 1/2 cup of potatoes, cubed
- 1/2 cup of celery, sliced, 1/2 cup of onions, diced
- 1 tablespoon olive oil, 1/4 teaspoon black pepper
- 1/4 teaspoon dried rosemary, 1 bay leaf

Directions:

1. Heat olive oil in a large pot over medium heat. Add the beef and cook for 5-7 minutes until browned on all sides.

2. Add the onions, carrots, potatoes, and celery, and sauté for another 5 minutes.

3. Pour in the beef broth, black pepper, rosemary, and bay leaf. Bring it to a boil, then reduce heat to a simmer and cook for 45-60 minutes, or until the beef is tender and the vegetables are cooked through. Remove the bay leaf before serving and enjoy warmth.

Nutritional Information per serving: 300 calories, 25g protein,

25g carbohydrates, 10g total fat, 4g fiber, 60mg cholesterol, 150mg sodium, 600mg potassium, 4g sugars,

220 mg phosphorus.

58. Butternut Squash and Apple Soup

Yield: 4 servings | **Prep time**: 10 minutes | **Cook time**: 30 minutes

Ingredients:

- 1 medium butternut squash, peeled and cubed
- 1 medium apple, peeled and chopped, 1 small onion, chopped, 1 tablespoon olive oil
- 4 cups low-sodium vegetable broth
- 1/4 teaspoon ground cinnamon, 1/4 teaspoon black pepper

Directions:

1. In a large pot, heat olive oil over medium heat. Add the onion and sauté for 5 minutes until softened.

2. Add the butternut squash, apple, vegetable broth, cinnamon, and black pepper.

3. Bring to a boil, then reduce the heat and simmer for 25-30 minutes, or until the squash is tender.

4. Use an immersion blender or transfer to a blender to puree the soup until smooth.

Nutritional Information per serving: 150 calories, 3g protein,

30g carbohydrates, 4g total fat, 5g fiber, 0mg cholesterol, 50mg sodium,

450mg potassium, 10g sugars,

90 mg phosphorus.

59. Lentil and Vegetable Soup

Yield: 4 servings | **Prep time**: 10 minutes | **Cook time**: 30 minutes

Ingredients:

- 1/2 cup dried lentils, rinsed
- 1/2 cup of carrots, diced
- 1/2 cup of celery, diced
- 1/4 cup of onions, diced
- 2 garlic cloves, minced
- 1 tablespoon olive oil
- 4 cups low-sodium vegetable broth, 1/4 teaspoon cumin
- 1/4 teaspoon black pepper, 1 bay leaf

Directions:

1. In a large pot, heat olive oil over medium heat. Sauté the onions, garlic, carrots, and celery for 5 minutes until softened.

2. Add the lentils, vegetable broth, cumin, black pepper, and bay leaf.

3. Bring to a boil, then reduce the heat and simmer for 25-30 minutes, or until the lentils are tender. Remove the bay leaves and serve warm.

Nutritional Information per serving: 180 calories, 10g protein,

30g carbohydrates, 4g total fat, 8g fiber, 0mg cholesterol, 60mg sodium,

400mg potassium, 4g sugars,

180 mg phosphorus.

60. Hearty Chicken and Rice Soup

Yield: 4 servings | **Prep time**: 10 minutes | **Cook time**: 30 minutes

Ingredients:

- 1 boneless, skinless chicken breast, cubed
- 1/2 cup cooked white rice
- 4 cups low-sodium chicken broth
- 1/2 cup of carrots, diced
- 1/2 cup of celery, diced
- 1/4 cup of onions, diced
- 1 tablespoon olive oil
- 1/4 teaspoon black pepper, 1/4 teaspoon garlic powder

Directions:

1. In a large pot, heat olive oil over medium heat. Sauté the onions, carrots, and celery for 5 minutes until softened.

2. Add the cubed chicken and cook for another 5 minutes until browned.

3. Stir in the chicken broth, rice, black pepper, and garlic powder. Bring to boil, then reduce heat and simmer for 20-25 minutes until the chicken is fully cooked.

Nutritional Information per serving: 220 calories, 18g protein,

22g carbohydrates, 7g total fat, 2g fiber, 40mg cholesterol, 140mg sodium, 300mg potassium, 2g sugars,

150 mg phosphorus.

61. Potato Leek Soup (Low Potassium)

Yield: 4 servings | **Prep time**: 10 minutes | **Cook time**: 30 minutes

Ingredients:

- 2 medium potatoes, peeled and diced (pre-soaked in water to reduce potassium)
- 2 medium leeks, white part only, sliced, 1 tablespoon olive oil
- 4 cups low-sodium vegetable broth
- 1/4 teaspoon black pepper, 1/4 teaspoon thyme

Directions:

1. In a large pot, heat olive oil over medium heat. Add the sliced leeks and sauté for 5 minutes until softened.
2. Add the diced potatoes, vegetable broth, black pepper, and thyme.
3. Bring to a boil, then reduce the heat and simmer for 25-30 minutes, or until the potatoes are tender.
4. Use an immersion blender to puree the soup until smooth. Serve warm, garnished with fresh herbs if desired.

Nutritional Information per serving: 150 calories, 3g protein,

30g carbohydrates, 4g total fat, 4g fiber, 0mg cholesterol, 50mg sodium,

350mg potassium, 2g sugars,

100 mg phosphorus.

62. Low-Sodium Minestrone Soup

Yield: 4 servings | **Prep time**: 10 minutes | **Cook time**: 30 minutes

Ingredients:

- 1/2 cup of whole wheat pasta
- 1/2 cup of carrots, diced, 1/2 cup of zucchini, diced, 1/2 cup kidney beans. , 1/4 cup celery, diced, 1/4 cup of onions, diced
- 4 cups low-sodium vegetable broth, 1 can diced tomatoes, 1 tablespoon olive oil
- 1/4 teaspoon black pepper. 1/4 teaspoon dried oregano, 1 bay leaf

Directions:

1. In a large pot, heat olive oil over medium heat. Sauté the onions, celery, and carrots for 5 minutes
2. Add the vegetable broth, diced tomatoes, black pepper, oregano, and bay leaf. Bring to a boil, then reduce the heat and simmer for 15 minutes.
3. Stir in the pasta, zucchini, and kidney beans. Simmer for 10 minutes until the pasta is cooked and the vegetables are tender.

Nutritional Information per serving: 220 calories, 8g protein,

40g carbohydrates, 6g total fat, 6g fiber, 0mg cholesterol, 120mg sodium,

500mg potassium, 5g sugars,

160 mg phosphorus.

63. Spinach and Quinoa Soup

Yield: 4 servings | **Prep time**: 10 minutes | **Cook time**: 20 minutes

Ingredients:

- 1/2 cup quinoa, rinsed
- 4 cups low-sodium vegetable broth
- 2 cups of fresh spinach, chopped
- 1 small onion, diced
- 1 garlic clove, minced
- 1 tablespoon olive oil
- 1/4 teaspoon black pepper
- 1/4 teaspoon ground cumin

Directions:

1. Heat olive oil in a large pot over medium heat. Add onions and garlic and sauté for 5 minutes until softened.

2. Add the quinoa, vegetable broth, black pepper, and cumin. Bring to a boil, then reduce heat and simmer for 15 minutes until the quinoa is cooked.

3. Stir in the chopped spinach and cook for another 2-3 minutes until wilted.

Nutritional Information per serving: 170 calories, 6g protein,

25g carbohydrates, 5g total fat, 4g fiber, 0mg cholesterol, 60mg sodium,

450mg potassium, 3g sugars,

170 mg phosphorus.

64. Broccoli and Cheese Soup

Yield: 4 servings | **Prep time**: 10 minutes | **Cook time**: 20 minutes

Ingredients:

- 2 cups of broccoli florets
- 1 small onion, diced, 1 garlic clove, minced, 1 tablespoon olive oil
- 4 cups low-sodium vegetable broth, 1/2 cup unsweetened almond milk, 1/2 cup shredded low-fat cheddar cheese
- 1/4 teaspoon black pepper, 1/4 teaspoon garlic powder

Directions:

1. Heat olive oil in a large pot over medium heat. Add the onion and garlic and sauté for 5 minutes.

2. Add the broccoli florets, vegetable broth, black pepper, and garlic powder. Bring to a boil, then reduce heat and simmer for 15 minutes until the broccoli is tender.

3. Use an immersion blender to puree the soup until smooth. Stir in the almond milk and shredded cheddar cheese, cook for another 2-3 minutes.

Nutritional Information per serving: 180 calories, 8g protein,

15g carbohydrates, 10g total fat, 4g fiber, 15mg cholesterol, 90mg sodium,

350mg potassium, 2g sugars,

200 mg phosphorus.

65. Tomato and Basil Soup

Yield: 4 servings | **Prep time**: 10 minutes | **Cook time**: 20 minutes

Ingredients:

- 1 can (15 oz) diced tomatoes (no added salt)
- 1 small onion, diced
- 1 garlic clove, minced
- 1 tablespoon olive oil
- 4 cups low-sodium vegetable broth
- 1/4 cup fresh basil, chopped
- 1/4 teaspoon black pepper
- 1/4 teaspoon dried oregano

Directions:

1. Heat olive oil in a large pot over medium heat. Add the onion and garlic and sauté for 5 minutes until softened.

2. Stir in the diced tomatoes, vegetable broth, black pepper, and oregano. Bring to a boil, then reduce heat and simmer for 15 minutes.

3. Use an immersion blender to puree the soup until smooth.

4. Stir in the fresh basil and cook for another 2 minutes.

5. Serve warm, optionally garnished with additional fresh basil.

Nutritional Information per serving: 120 calories, 3g protein,

18g carbohydrates, 5g total fat, 4g fiber, 0mg cholesterol, 60mg sodium,

400mg potassium, 6g sugars,

60 mg phosphorus.

Chapter 6:

Vegetarian and Vegan Options

66. Vegan Stir-Fry with Tofu

Yield: 2 servings | **Prep time**: 10 minutes | **Cook time**: 10 minutes

Ingredients:

- 1/2 block firm tofu, pressed and cubed, 1/2 cup broccoli florets

- 1/2 cup bell peppers, sliced, 1/2 cup carrots, sliced, 1 tablespoon olive oil

- 1 tablespoon low-sodium soy sauce, 1 tablespoon rice vinegar

- 1 teaspoon fresh ginger, minced, 1 garlic clove, minced

- 1/4 teaspoon black pepper

Directions:

1. Heat olive oil in a large skillet over medium heat. Add the cubed tofu and cook for 5-7 minutes until golden brown on all sides.

2. Remove the tofu from the skillet and set aside. In the same skillet, add the broccoli, bell peppers, carrots, ginger, and garlic. Sauté for 3-4 minutes until the vegetables are tender.

3. Return the tofu to the skillet and add soy sauce, rice vinegar, and black pepper. Stir well and cook for another 2 minutes.

Nutritional Information per serving: 220 calories, 10g protein,

15g carbohydrates, 14g total fat, 4g fiber, 0mg cholesterol, 150mg sodium,

400mg potassium, 5g sugars,

200 mg phosphorus.

67. Black Bean and Rice Casserole

Yield: 4 servings | **Prep time**: 10 minutes | **Cook time**: 30 minutes

Ingredients:

- 1 cup cooked brown rice

- 1 can (15 oz) black beans, rinsed and drained

- 1/2 cup of diced tomatoes, 1/2 cup diced bell peppers

- 1/4 cup of diced onions

- 1 tablespoon olive oil, 1 teaspoon cumin

- 1/4 teaspoon black pepper

Directions:

1. Preheat the oven to 350°F

2. In a large skillet, heat olive oil over medium heat. Sauté the onions, bell peppers, and tomatoes for 5 minutes until softened. Add the black beans, cumin, black pepper, and cooked brown rice. Stir well to combine.

3. Transfer the mixture to a baking dish. Top with shredded cheese if desired. Bake for 20-25 minutes, or until heated through and the cheese melted.

Nutritional Information per serving: 250 calories, 10g protein,

40g carbohydrates, 7g total fat, 8g fiber, 0mg cholesterol, 150mg sodium,

450mg potassium, 3g sugars,

180 mg phosphorus.

68. Lentil Shepherd's Pie

Yield: 4 servings | **Prep time**: 15 minutes | **Cook time**: 30 minutes

Ingredients:

- 1 cup dried lentils, rinsed, 4 cups low-sodium vegetable broth, 2 medium potatoes, peeled and diced, 1/2 cup of carrots, diced

- 1/2 cup of peas ,1/4 cup of onions, diced, 1 tablespoon olive oil, 1/4 teaspoon black pepper, 1/4 teaspoon thyme, 1/4 cup unsweetened almond milk

Directions:

1. In a pot, bring the lentils and vegetable broth to a boil. Reduce heat and simmer for 20 minutes or until the lentils are tender. Drain any excess liquid and set aside.

2. Boil the diced potatoes until tender, 10-12 minutes. Drain, mash the potatoes, and mix with almond milk and black pepper.

3. Preheat the oven to 350°F. In a skillet, heat olive oil over medium heat. Sauté the onions and carrots for 5 minutes. Spread the lentil mixture in a baking dish and top with the mashed potatoes, spreading evenly. Bake for 20 minutes.

Nutritional Information per serving: 280 calories, 12g protein,

45g carbohydrates, 6g total fat, 10g fiber, 0mg cholesterol, 100mg sodium,

650mg potassium, 5g sugars,

250 mg phosphorus.

69. Roasted Vegetable Quinoa Bowl

Yield: 2 servings | **Prep time**: 10 minutes | **Cook time**: 20 minutes

Ingredients:

- 1/2 cup quinoa, rinsed, 1 cup of water, 1 small zucchini, sliced, 1 red bell pepper, sliced

- 1/2 cup cherry tomatoes, halved, 1 tablespoon olive oil, 1 tablespoon of balsamic vinegar

- 1/4 teaspoon black pepper, 1/4 teaspoon dried oregano

Directions:

1. Preheat the oven to 400°F. In a pot, bring the quinoa and water to a boil. Reduce heat and simmer for 15 minutes, or until the quinoa is tender and water is absorbed. Fluff with a fork and set aside.

2. Toss the zucchini, bell pepper, and cherry tomatoes with olive oil, balsamic vinegar, black pepper, and oregano. Spread the vegetables on a baking sheet and roast for 15-20 minutes.

3. In serving bowls, divide the cooked quinoa and top with the roasted vegetables. Garnish with fresh parsley if desired.

Nutritional Information per serving: 250 calories, 7g protein,

35g carbohydrates, 9g total fat, 5g fiber, 0mg cholesterol, 70mg sodium,

450mg potassium, 6g sugars,

180 mg phosphorus.

70. Stuffed Bell Peppers with Lentils

Yield: 2 servings | **Prep time**: 10 minutes | **Cook time**: 25 minutes

Ingredients:

- 2 large bell peppers (any color), halved and seeds removed
- 1/2 cup cooked lentils
- 1/4 cup of diced tomatoes, 1/4 cup of diced onions
- 1 tablespoon olive oil
- 1/4 teaspoon cumin, 1/4 teaspoon black pepper

Directions:

1. Preheat the oven to 375°F. In a skillet, heat olive oil over medium heat. Sauté the onions for 3-4 minutes until softened. Add the cooked lentils, diced tomatoes, cumin, and black pepper. Cook for another 5 minutes.

2. Stuff the bell pepper halves with the lentil mixture. Place the stuffed peppers in a baking dish.

3. Cover the dish with foil and bake for 20-25 minutes, or until the peppers are tender. Garnish with fresh parsley if desired and serve warm.

Nutritional Information per serving: 200 calories, 8g protein,

30g carbohydrates, 6g total fat, 8g fiber, 0mg cholesterol, 80mg sodium,

500mg potassium, 6g sugars,

220 mg phosphorus.

71. Cauliflower Tacos with Cilantro-Lime Dressing

Yield: 2 servings | **Prep time**: 10 minutes | **Cook time**: 15 minutes

Ingredients:

- 1 small cauliflower, cut into florets, 1 tablespoon olive oil
- 1/4 teaspoon black pepper, 1/4 teaspoon paprika, 4 small corn tortillas, 1/4 cup shredded lettuce

For the Cilantro-Lime Dressing:

- 1/4 cup plain Greek yogurt, 1 tablespoon lime juice, 1 tablespoon fresh cilantro, chopped, 1/4 teaspoon garlic powder

Directions:

1. Preheat the oven to 400°F Toss the cauliflower florets with olive oil, black pepper, and paprika. Spread on a baking sheet and roast for 15-20 minutes.

2. In a small bowl, mix the yogurt, lime juice, cilantro, and garlic powder to make the dressing.

3. Warm the corn tortillas in a skillet or microwave. Assemble the tacos by adding roasted cauliflower, shredded lettuce.

Nutritional Information per serving: 250 calories, 6g protein,

32g carbohydrates, 10g total fat, 7g fiber, 0mg cholesterol, 80mg sodium,

400mg potassium, 4g sugars,

130 mg phosphorus.

72. Vegan Bean Chili

Yield: 4 servings | **Prep time**: 10 minutes | **Cook time**: 30 minutes

Ingredients:

- 1 can (15 oz) black beans, rinsed and drained

- 1 can (15 oz) kidney beans, rinsed and drained

- 1 can (15 oz) diced tomatoes (no added salt), 1/4 cup of diced onions, 1/4 cup diced bell peppers

- 1 tablespoon olive oil, 1 tablespoon chili powder, 1 teaspoon cumin

- 1/4 teaspoon black pepper, 1/4 teaspoon garlic powder

Directions:

1. In a large pot, heat olive oil over medium heat. Sauté the onions and peppers for 5 minutes until softened.

2. Add the black beans, kidney beans, diced tomatoes, chili powder, cumin, black pepper, and garlic powder.

3. Bring the mixture to a boil, then reduce heat and simmer for 20-25 minutes, stirring occasionally.

Nutritional Information per serving: 250 calories, 12g protein,

40g carbohydrates, 6g total fat, 10g fiber, 0mg cholesterol, 150mg sodium,

550mg potassium, 5g sugars,

220 mg phosphorus.

73. Grilled Portobello Mushrooms

Yield: 2 servings | **Prep time**: 5 minutes | **Cook time**: 10 minutes

Ingredients:

- 2 large Portobello mushroom caps

- 1 tablespoon olive oil

- 1 tablespoon of balsamic vinegar

- 1/4 teaspoon garlic powder

- 1/4 teaspoon black pepper

- 1 tablespoon fresh parsley, chopped (optional)

Directions:

1. Preheat the grill or a grill pan to medium-high heat.

2. In a small bowl, mix the olive oil, balsamic vinegar, garlic powder, and black pepper. Brush both sides of the mushroom caps with the mixture.

3. Grill the mushrooms for 4-5 minutes on each side until tender and slightly charred.

4. Garnish with fresh parsley if desired and serve as a side dish or burger substitute.

Nutritional Information per serving: 120 calories, 3g protein,

10g carbohydrates, 8g total fat, 2g fiber, 0mg cholesterol, 60mg sodium,

300mg potassium, 3g sugars,

120 mg phosphorus.

74. Kidney-Friendly Tempeh Stir-Fry

Yield: 2 servings | **Prep time**: 10 minutes | **Cook time**: 10 minutes

Ingredients:

- 1/2 block tempeh, cubed, 1/2 cup broccoli florets, 1/2 cup bell peppers, sliced

- 1/4 cup carrots, sliced, 1 tablespoon olive oil

- 1 tablespoon low-sodium soy sauce, 1 tablespoon rice vinegar

- 1 teaspoon fresh ginger, minced, 1 garlic clove, minced

- 1/4 teaspoon black pepper

Directions:

1. Heat olive oil in a large skillet over medium heat. Add the cubed tempeh and cook for 5-7 minutes until golden brown.

2. Remove the tempeh from the skillet and set aside. In the same skillet, sauté the broccoli, bell peppers, carrots, ginger, and garlic for 3-4 minutes until tender.

3. Return the tempeh to the skillet and stir in the soy sauce, rice vinegar, and black pepper. Cook for another 2 minutes, stirring well.

Nutritional Information per serving: 240 calories, 13g protein,

20g carbohydrates, 12g total fat, 5g fiber, 0mg cholesterol, 200mg sodium,

450mg potassium, 4g sugars,

210 mg phosphorus.

75. Baked Sweet Potato with Avocado

Yield: 2 servings | **Prep time**: 5 minutes | **Cook time**: 45 minutes

Ingredients:

- 2 small, sweet potatoes

- 1 ripe avocado

- 1 tablespoon lime juice

- 1/4 teaspoon garlic powder

- 1/4 teaspoon black pepper

Directions:

1. Preheat the oven to 400°F (200°C). Wash the sweet potatoes and pierce them several times with a fork.

2. Place the sweet potatoes on a baking sheet and bake for 40-45 minutes, or until tender.

3. While the sweet potatoes are baking, mash the avocado in a bowl and mix with lime juice, garlic powder, and black pepper.

4. Once the sweet potatoes are done, slice them open and top with the mashed avocado mixture. Garnish with cilantro if desired.

5. Serve warm.

Nutritional Information per serving: 280 calories, 5g protein,

45g carbohydrates, 12g total fat, 10g fiber, 0mg cholesterol, 15mg sodium, 750mg potassium, 7g sugars,

90 mg phosphorus.

76. Tofu Scramble with Vegetables

Yield: 2 servings | **Prep time**: 10 minutes | **Cook time**: 10 minutes

Ingredients:

- 1/2 block firm tofu, crumbled
- 1/4 cup of diced onions
- 1/4 cup diced bell peppers
- 1/4 cup of spinach, chopped
- 1 tablespoon olive oil, 1/4 teaspoon turmeric
- 1/4 teaspoon black pepper, 1/4 teaspoon garlic powder

Directions:

1. Heat olive oil in a skillet over medium heat. Add the onions and bell peppers, sautéing for 3-4 minutes until softened.

2. Add the crumbled tofu, turmeric, black pepper, and garlic powder to the skillet. Cook for 5-7 minutes, stirring occasionally, until the tofu is lightly browned.

3. Stir in the chopped spinach and cook for another 2 minutes until wilted.

4. Garnish with fresh parsley if desired and serve warm.

Nutritional Information per serving: 180 calories, 10g protein,

10g carbohydrates, 12g total fat, 3g fiber, 0mg cholesterol, 120mg sodium,

300mg potassium, 2g sugars,

170 mg phosphorus.

77. Quinoa and Black Bean Salad

Yield: 4 servings | **Prep time**: 10 minutes | **Cook time**: 15 minutes

Ingredients:

- 1/2 cup of quinoa, rinsed, 1 cup of water
- 1 can (15 oz) black beans, rinsed and drained
- 1/2 cup corn kernels, 1/2 cup of diced tomatoes
- 1 tablespoon olive oil, 1 tablespoon lime juice
- 1 tablespoon fresh cilantro, chopped
- 1/4 teaspoon cumin, 1/4 teaspoon black pepper

Directions:

1. In a pot, bring the quinoa and water to a boil. Reduce heat and simmer for 15 minutes, or until the quinoa is tender and water is absorbed. Fluff with a fork and set aside.

2. In a large bowl, combine the cooked quinoa, black beans, corn, diced tomatoes, olive oil, lime juice, cilantro, cumin, and black pepper. Toss well to combine.

Nutritional Information per serving: 250 calories, 10g protein,

40g carbohydrates, 7g total fat, 8g fiber, 0mg cholesterol, 150mg sodium,

450mg potassium, 3g sugars,

180 mg phosphorus.

78. Zucchini and Carrot Fritters

Yield: 4 servings | **Prep time**: 10 minutes | **Cook time**: 10 minutes

Ingredients:

- 1 medium zucchini, grated
- 1 medium carrot, grated
- 1/4 cup all-purpose flour
- 1 large egg white
- 1 tablespoon olive oil
- 1/4 teaspoon garlic powder
- 1/4 teaspoon black pepper
- 1 tablespoon fresh parsley, chopped (optional)

Directions:

1. Place the grated zucchini and carrot in a clean kitchen towel and squeeze out excess moisture.

2. In a bowl, mix the zucchini, carrot, flour, egg white, garlic powder, black pepper, and parsley until well combined.

3. Heat olive oil in a skillet over medium heat. Drop spoonful of the mixture into the skillet and flatten slightly with a spatula.

4. Cook for 3-4 minutes on each side, or until golden brown and crispy.

5. Serve warm as a side dish or snack.

Nutritional Information per serving: 120 calories, 4g protein,

15g carbohydrates, 6g total fat, 3g fiber, 0mg cholesterol, 90mg sodium,

250mg potassium, 3g sugars,

100 mg phosphorus.

Chapter 7:

Desserts

79. Low-Sugar Baked Apple Slices

Yield: 2 servings | **Prep time**: 5 minutes | **Cook time**: 20 minutes

Ingredients:

- 2 medium apples, sliced
- 1 tablespoon cinnamon
- 1 tablespoon honey (optional)
- 1/4 teaspoon nutmeg

Directions:

1. Preheat the oven to 375°F (190°C).
2. Arrange the apple slices on a baking sheet lined with parchment paper.
3. Sprinkle the cinnamon and nutmeg over the apple slices, and drizzle honey if desired.
4. Bake for 15-20 minutes, or until the apples are tender and slightly caramelized.
5. Serve warm, optionally with a dollop of Greek yogurt.

Nutritional Information per serving: 100 calories, 1g protein,

25g carbohydrates, 0g total fat,

5g fiber, 0mg cholesterol, 0mg sodium, 200mg potassium, 18g sugars,

20 mg phosphorus.

80. Blueberry Oatmeal Bars

Yield: 6 servings | **Prep time**: 10 minutes | **Cook time**: 30 minutes

Ingredients:

- 1 cup rolled oats
- 1/2 cup whole wheat flour
- 1/4 cup unsweetened applesauce
- 1 tablespoon honey
- 1/2 cup fresh or frozen blueberries
- 1/4 teaspoon cinnamon
- 1/4 teaspoon vanilla extract

Directions:

1. Preheat the oven to 350°F (175°C). Grease an 8-inch square baking dish.
2. In a bowl, combine the oats, flour, applesauce, honey, cinnamon, and vanilla extract. Mix well.
3. Gently fold in the blueberries.
4. Press the mixture evenly into the baking dish.
5. Bake for 25-30 minutes, or until the top is golden brown.
6. Let's cool before cutting into bars.

Nutritional Information per serving: 120 calories, 3g protein,

22g carbohydrates, 2g total fat, 3g fiber, 0mg cholesterol, 5mg sodium,

150mg potassium, 8g sugars,

50 mg phosphorus

81. Cinnamon-Spiced Pear Crisp

Yield: 4 servings | **Prep time**: 10 minutes | **Cook time**: 30 minutes

Ingredients:

- 3 medium pears, sliced, 1/4 cup of rolled oats
- 1/4 cup of whole wheat flour
- 1 tablespoon honey, 1 tablespoon unsweetened applesauce
- 1 teaspoon cinnamon, 1/4 teaspoon nutmeg

Directions:

1. Preheat the oven to 350°F Grease a small baking dish.
2. Arrange the sliced pears at the bottom of the dish.
3. In a bowl, combine the oats, flour, honey, applesauce, cinnamon, and nutmeg. Mix well to form a crumbly topping.
4. Sprinkle the topping evenly over the pears.
5. Bake for 25-30 minutes, or until the pears are tender and the topping is golden brown.
6. Serve warm.

Nutritional Information per serving: 150 calories, 2g protein,

35g carbohydrates, 2g total fat, 6g fiber, 0mg cholesterol, 5mg sodium,

200mg potassium, 15g sugars,

40 mg phosphorus.

82. Coconut Chia Seed Pudding

Yield: 2 servings | **Prep time**: 5 minutes | **Cook time**: 0 minutes (refrigeration time: 4 hours)

Ingredients:

- 1/2 cup unsweetened coconut milk
- 2 tablespoons chia seeds
- 1 tablespoon honey (optional)
- 1/4 teaspoon vanilla extract
- 1/4 cup shredded coconut (optional, for topping)

Directions:

1. In a bowl, whisk together the coconut milk, chia seeds, honey, and vanilla extract.
2. Cover and refrigerate for at least 4 hours, or overnight, until the mixture thickens into a pudding-like consistency.
3. Serve topped with shredded coconut if desired.

Nutritional Information per serving: 160 calories, 4g protein,

15g carbohydrates, 9g total fat, 8g fiber, 0mg cholesterol, 10mg sodium,

150mg potassium, 8g sugars,

140 mg phosphorus.

83. Vanilla Greek Yogurt with Berries

Yield: 2 servings | **Prep time**: 5 minutes | **Cook time**: 0 minutes

Ingredients:

- 1 cup plain Greek yogurt
- 1/2 teaspoon vanilla extract
- 1 tablespoon honey (optional)
- 1/2 cup mixed fresh berries (such as strawberries, blueberries, or raspberries)

Directions:

1. In a bowl, mix the Greek yogurt with vanilla extract and honey (if using).
2. Divide the yogurt into two bowls and top with fresh berries.
3. Serve immediately as a light dessert or snack.

Nutritional Information per serving: 120 calories, 10g protein,

18g carbohydrates, 1g total fat, 0g fiber, 0mg cholesterol, 50mg sodium,

200mg potassium, 12g sugars,

110 mg phosphorus.

84. Low-Sugar Banana Bread

Yield: 8 servings | **Prep time**: 10 minutes | **Cook time**: 50 minutes

Ingredients:

- 3 ripe bananas, mashed
- 1/4 cup unsweetened applesauce, 1/4 cup of honey, 1 large egg
- 1 teaspoon vanilla extract, 1 1/2 cups of whole wheat flour, 1 teaspoon of baking soda
- 1/2 teaspoon cinnamon, 1/4 teaspoon salt

Directions:

1. Preheat the oven to 350°F. Grease a loaf pan. In a large bowl, combine the mashed bananas, applesauce, honey, egg, and vanilla extract. Mix well. In a separate bowl, whisk together the flour, baking soda, cinnamon.
2. Gradually add the dry ingredients to the wet ingredients, stirring until just combined.
3. Pour the batter into the prepared loaf pan and bake for 45-50 minutes, or until a toothpick inserted into the center comes out clean. Let the banana bread cool before slicing and serving.

Nutritional Information per serving: 180 calories, 4g protein,

35g carbohydrates, 3g total fat, 4g fiber, 20mg cholesterol, 150mg sodium, 300mg potassium, 12g sugars,

60 mg phosphorus.

85. Rice Pudding with Cinnamon

Yield: 4 servings | **Prep time**: 5 minutes | **Cook time**: 25 minutes

Ingredients:

- 1/2 cup uncooked white rice
- 2 cups of unsweetened almond milk
- 1 tablespoon honey (optional)
- 1 teaspoon vanilla extract
- 1/2 teaspoon ground cinnamon

Directions:

1. In a medium saucepan, combine the rice and almond milk. Bring to a boil, then reduce the heat and simmer for 20-25 minutes, stirring occasionally, until the rice is tender, and the mixture thickens.
2. Stir in the honey (if using), vanilla extract, and cinnamon.
3. Serve warm or chilled, garnished with a sprinkle of cinnamon.

Nutritional Information per serving: 150 calories, 3g protein,

30g carbohydrates, 2g total fat, 1g fiber, 0mg cholesterol, 40mg sodium,

100mg potassium, 8g sugars,

50 mg phosphorus.

86. Strawberry Sorbet

Yield: 4 servings | **Prep time**: 5 minutes | **Cook time**: 0 minutes (freezing time: 4 hours)

Ingredients:

- 2 cups fresh strawberries, hulled
- 1/4 cup of honey (or maple syrup)
- 1 tablespoon lemon juice

Directions:

1. In a blender or food processor, blend the strawberries, honey, and lemon juice until smooth.
2. Pour the mixture into a shallow dish and freeze for 4 hours, stirring every hour to break up ice crystals.
3. Once fully frozen, scoop and serve as a light, refreshing dessert.

Nutritional Information per serving:

80 calories, 1g protein,

20g carbohydrates, 0g total fat, 3g fiber, 0mg cholesterol, 0mg sodium,

150mg potassium, 15g sugars,

20 mg phosphorus.

87. Apple Cinnamon Muffins

Yield: 6 muffins | **Prep time**: 10 minutes | **Cook time**: 20 minutes

Ingredients:

- 1 cup whole wheat flour

- 1/2 cup unsweetened applesauce

- 1 large egg, 1/4 cup of honey, 1 teaspoon cinnamon

- 1/2 teaspoon of baking powder, 1/2 teaspoon baking soda

- 1/2 teaspoon vanilla extract, 1 medium apple, diced

Directions:

1. Preheat the oven to 350°F and line a muffin tin with paper liners.

2. In a large bowl, mix the applesauce, egg, honey, and vanilla extract. In another bowl, combine the flour, cinnamon, baking powder, and baking soda.

3. Gradually add the dry ingredients to the wet ingredients, mixing until just combined. Fold in the diced apple.

4. Divide the batter evenly among the muffin cups and bake for 18-20 minutes, or until a toothpick inserted into the center comes out clean.

Nutritional Information per serving: 120 calories, 3g protein,

25g carbohydrates, 2g total fat, 2g fiber, 20mg cholesterol, 100mg sodium, 150mg potassium, 12g sugars,

40 mg phosphorus.

88. Lemon Yogurt Parfait

Yield: 2 servings | **Prep time**: 5 minutes | **Cook time**: 0 minutes

Ingredients:

- 1 cup plain Greek yogurt

- 1 tablespoon honey

- 1 teaspoon lemon zest

- 1/2 teaspoon vanilla extract

- 1/4 cup granola (low sodium)

- 1/4 cup fresh berries (optional)

Directions:

1. In a bowl, mix the Greek yogurt with honey, lemon zest, and vanilla extract until well combined.

2. Divide the yogurt mixture into two bowls or glasses.

3. Top each serving with granola and fresh berries if desired.

4. Serve immediately as a refreshing dessert or snack.

Nutritional Information per serving: 180 calories, 10g protein,

28g carbohydrates, 3g total fat, 1g fiber, 0mg cholesterol, 60mg sodium,

200mg potassium, 15g sugars,

100 mg phosphorus.

89. Baked Peaches with Almonds

Yield: 2 servings | **Prep time**: 5 minutes | **Cook time**: 15 minutes

Ingredients:

- 2 ripe peaches, halved and pitted
- 2 tablespoons slivered almonds
- 1 tablespoon honey
- 1/2 teaspoon cinnamon

Directions:

1. Preheat the oven to 375°F (190°C).
2. Place the peach halves cut side up on a baking sheet. Drizzle with honey and sprinkle with cinnamon.
3. Top each peach with slivered almonds.
4. Bake for 12-15 minutes, or until the peaches are tender.
5. Serve warm, optionally with a dollop of Greek yogurt.

Nutritional Information per serving: 130 calories, 3g protein,

24g carbohydrates, 5g total fat, 3g fiber, 0mg cholesterol, 0mg sodium,

300mg potassium, 18g sugars,

60 mg phosphorus.

90. Dark Chocolate Avocado Mousse

Yield: 2 servings | **Prep time**: 5 minutes | **Cook time**: 0 minutes

Ingredients:

- 1 ripe avocado
- 2 tablespoons unsweetened cocoa powder
- 2 tablespoons honey
- 1/4 teaspoon vanilla extract
- 1 tablespoon almond milk (unsweetened)

Directions:

1. In a blender or food processor, combine the avocado, cocoa powder, honey, vanilla extract, and almond milk.
2. Blend until smooth and creamy.
3. Chill in the refrigerator for at least 30 minutes before serving.
4. Optionally, garnish with fresh berries or a sprinkle of coconut flakes.

Nutritional Information per serving: 180 calories, 3g protein,

25g carbohydrates, 9g total fat, 7g fiber, 0mg cholesterol, 10mg sodium,

450mg potassium, 12g sugars,

100 mg phosphorus.

91. Pineapple Coconut Sorbet

Yield: 4 servings | **Prep time**: 5 minutes | **Cook time**: 0 minutes (freezing time: 4 hours)

Ingredients:

- 2 cups of fresh pineapple chunks
- 1/2 cup unsweetened coconut milk
- 1 tablespoon honey (optional)
- 1 tablespoon lime juice

Directions:

1. In a blender or food processor, blend the pineapple chunks, coconut milk, honey (if using), and lime juice until smooth.

2. Pour the mixture into a shallow dish and freeze for 4 hours, stirring every hour to break up ice crystals.

3. Once fully frozen, scoop and serve as a refreshing dessert.

Nutritional Information per serving:

90 calories, 1g protein,

20g carbohydrates, 2g total fat, 2g fiber, 0mg cholesterol, 5mg sodium,

200mg potassium, 12g sugars,

30 mg phosphorus.

Chapter 8:

Beverages

92. Herbal Tea Blends

Yield: 2 servings | **Prep time**: 5 minutes | **Cook time**: 5 minutes

Ingredients:

- 2 cups of water
- 1 teaspoon dried chamomile flowers
- 1 teaspoon dried peppermint leaves
- 1 teaspoon dried lavender buds
- 1 teaspoon honey (optional)
- Lemon slices (optional)

Directions:

1. In a small saucepan, bring the water to a boil.
2. Remove from heat and add the chamomile, peppermint, and lavender. Let steep for 5 minutes.
3. Strain the tea into cups and sweeten with honey if desired.
4. Serve with lemon slices for an added citrus flavor.

Nutritional Information per serving:

10 calories, 0g protein,

2g carbohydrates, 0g total fat, 0g fiber, 0mg cholesterol, 0mg sodium,

20mg potassium, 2g sugars,

0 mg phosphorus.

93. Green Smoothie with Kale and Pineapple

Yield: 2 servings | **Prep time**: 5 minutes | **Cook time**: 0 minutes

Ingredients:

- 1 cup fresh kale leaves (stems removed)
- 1/2 cup fresh pineapple chunks
- 1/2 banana
- 1/2 cup unsweetened almond milk
- 1/2 cup of water
- 1 tablespoon chia seeds (optional)

Directions:

1. In a blender, combine the kale, pineapple, banana, almond milk, water, and chia seeds (if using).
2. Blend until smooth and creamy.
3. Serve immediately for a refreshing and nutrient-packed drink.

Nutritional Information per serving: 120 calories, 3g protein,

25g carbohydrates, 3g total fat, 5g fiber, 0mg cholesterol, 40mg sodium,

400mg potassium, 12g sugars,

50 mg phosphorus.

94. Cucumber and Lemon Water

Yield: 4 servings | **Prep time**: 5 minutes | **Cook time**: 0 minutes

Ingredients:

- 1 small cucumber, thinly sliced
- 1 lemon, thinly sliced
- 4 cups of water
- Fresh mint leaves (optional)

Directions:

1. In a large pitcher, combine sliced cucumber and lemon.
2. Add the water and stir gently.
3. Let the mixture sit in the refrigerator for at least 30 minutes to allow the flavors to infuse.
4. Serve chilled, garnished with fresh mint leaves if desired.

Nutritional Information per serving:

5 calories, 0g protein, 1g carbohydrates, 0g total fat, 0g fiber, 0mg cholesterol, 0mg sodium, 50mg potassium,

0g sugars, 5 mg phosphorus.

95. Kidney-Friendly Berry Smoothie

Yield: 2 servings | **Prep time**: 5 minutes | **Cook time**: 0 minutes

Ingredients:

- 1/2 cup fresh or frozen strawberries
- 1/2 cup fresh or frozen blueberries
- 1/2 cup unsweetened almond milk
- 1/2 cup of water
- 1 tablespoon chia seeds (optional)

Directions:

1. In a blender, combine the strawberries, blueberries, almond milk, water, and chia seeds (if using).
2. Blend until smooth and creamy.
3. Serve immediately as a light, kidney-friendly beverage.

Nutritional Information per serving: 100 calories, 2g protein,

20g carbohydrates, 3g total fat, 6g fiber, 0mg cholesterol, 30mg sodium,

200mg potassium, 10g sugars,

20 mg phosphorus.

96. Watermelon Mint Lemonade

Yield: 4 servings | **Prep time**: 5 minutes | **Cook time**: 0 minutes

Ingredients:

- 2 cups of watermelon chunks
- 1/4 cup fresh lemon juice
- 2 tablespoons of honey (optional)
- 4 cups of water
- Fresh mint leaves (for garnish)

Directions:

1. In a blender, blend the watermelon and lemon juice until smooth.
2. Strain the mixture through a fine mesh sieve to remove any pulp.
3. Stir in the water and honey (if using).
4. Serve chilled, garnished with fresh mint leaves.

Nutritional Information per serving:

40 calories, 1g protein, 10g carbohydrates, 0g total fat, 1g fiber,

0mg cholesterol, 5mg sodium, 100mg potassium, 8g sugars,

10 mg phosphorus.

97. Low-Sugar Cranberry Juice Blend

Yield: 4 servings | **Prep time**: 5 minutes | **Cook time**: 0 minutes

Ingredients:

- 1/2 cup 100% pure cranberry juice (unsweetened)
- 2 cups of water
- 1/4 cup fresh orange juice
- 1 tablespoon honey (optional)
- Fresh orange slices (optional, for garnish)

Directions:

1. In a large pitcher, mix the cranberry juice, water, and orange juice.
2. Stir in honey if you prefer a sweeter flavor.
3. Serve chilled, garnished with fresh orange slices if desired.

Nutritional Information per serving:

30 calories, 0g protein,

8g carbohydrates, 0g total fat, 0g fiber, 0mg cholesterol, 5mg sodium,

50mg potassium, 6g sugars,

5 mg phosphorus.

98. Iced Green Tea with Lemon

Yield: 4 servings | **Prep time**: 5 minutes | **Cook time**: 10 minutes

Ingredients:

- 4 green tea bags
- 4 cups of water
- 1 lemon, thinly sliced
- Ice cubes
- 1 tablespoon honey (optional)

Directions:

1. Bring the water to a boil, then remove from heat. Add the green tea bags and steep for 5 minutes.

2. Remove the tea bags and let the tea cool to room temperature.

3. Pour the tea into a pitcher, add lemon slices, and refrigerate until chilled.

4. Serve over ice, sweetened with honey if desired.

Nutritional Information per serving:

10 calories, 0g protein,

2g carbohydrates, 0g total fat, 0g fiber, 0mg cholesterol, 0mg sodium,

25mg potassium, 2g sugars,

0 mg phosphorus.

99. Ginger and Turmeric Detox Drink

Yield: 2 servings | **Prep time**: 5 minutes | **Cook time**: 5 minutes

Ingredients:

- 2 cups of water
- 1 teaspoon fresh ginger, grated
- 1/2 teaspoon ground turmeric
- 1 tablespoon lemon juice
- 1 tablespoon honey (optional)
- Ice cubes (optional)

Directions:

1. Bring the water to a boil, then remove from heat. Add grated ginger and turmeric.

2. Let the mixture steep for 5 minutes.

3. Strain the drink into glasses and stir in the lemon juice and honey if desired.

4. Serve warm or over ice for a refreshing detox drink.

Nutritional Information per serving:

20 calories, 0g protein,

5g carbohydrates, 0g total fat, 0g fiber, 0mg cholesterol, 5mg sodium,

50mg potassium, 4g sugars,

5 mg phosphorus.

100. Low-Sugar Almond Milk Smoothie

Yield: 2 servings | **Prep time**: 5 minutes | **Cook time**: 0 minutes

Ingredients:

- 1 cup unsweetened almond milk
- 1/2 banana
- 1/2 cup spinach
- 1/4 cup frozen berries
- 1 tablespoon chia seeds (optional)

Directions:

1. In a blender, combine the almond milk, banana, spinach, berries, and chia seeds (if using).
2. Blend until smooth and creamy.
3. Serve immediately as a light, nutritious smoothie.

Nutritional Information per serving:

90 calories, 3g protein,

15g carbohydrates, 3g total fat, 5g fiber, 0mg cholesterol, 80mg sodium,

300mg potassium, 8g sugars,

40 mg phosphorus.

101. Strawberry Lemonade

Yield: 4 servings | **Prep time**: 5 minutes | **Cook time**: 0 minutes

Ingredients:

- 1 cup fresh strawberries, hulled
- 1/4 cup fresh lemon juice
- 4 cups of water
- 1 tablespoon honey (optional)
- Ice cubes

Directions:

1. In a blender, puree the strawberries and lemon juice until smooth.
2. Strain the mixture to remove seeds and pulp if desired.
3. Stir in the water and honey (if using).
4. Serve over ice as a refreshing summer drink.

Nutritional Information per serving:

40 calories, 1g protein,

10g carbohydrates, 0g total fat, 1g fiber, 0mg cholesterol, 0mg sodium,

100mg potassium, 7g sugars,

10 mg phosphorus.

102. Cucumber and Basil Infused Water

Yield: 4 servings | **Prep time**: 5 minutes | **Cook time**: 0 minutes

Ingredients:

- 1 small cucumber, thinly sliced
- 1/4 cup fresh basil leaves
- 4 cups water
- Ice cubes

Directions:

1. In a large pitcher, combine the cucumber slices and fresh basil leaves.
2. Add the water and let the mixture sit in the refrigerator for at least 30 minutes to allow the flavors to infuse.
3. Serve chilled over ice.

Nutritional Information per serving:

5 calories, 0g protein, 1g carbohydrates, 0g total fat, 0g fiber, 0mg cholesterol, 0mg sodium, 30mg potassium,

0g sugars, 5 mg phosphorus.

103. Low-Potassium Vegetable Juice

Yield: 2 servings | **Prep time**: 10 minutes | **Cook time**: 0 minutes

Ingredients:

- 1/2 cup cucumber, chopped
- 1/2 cup of carrots, chopped
- 1/4 cup bell peppers, chopped
- 1/4 cup celery, chopped
- 1/2 cup water
- 1 tablespoon lemon juice

Directions:

1. In a blender, combine the cucumber, carrots, bell peppers, celery, water, and lemon juice.
2. Blend until smooth.
3. Strain the juice to remove any pulp if desired.
4. Serve immediately for a fresh, low-potassium vegetable drink.

Nutritional Information per serving:

40 calories, 1g protein,

9g carbohydrates, 0g total fat, 2g fiber, 0mg cholesterol, 15mg sodium,

200mg potassium, 5g sugars,

20 mg phosphorus.

104. Apple Cinnamon Iced Tea

Yield: 4 servings | **Prep time**: 5 minutes | **Cook time**: 10 minutes

Ingredients:

- 4 black tea bags
- 4 cups of water
- 1 apple, thinly sliced
- 1 cinnamon stick
- 1 tablespoon honey (optional)
- Ice cubes

Directions:

1. Bring the water to a boil, then remove from heat. Add the tea bags, sliced apple, and cinnamon stick, and steep for 5 minutes.

2. Remove the tea bags and let the tea cool to room temperature.

3. Remove the cinnamon stick and apple slices. Stir in honey if desired.

4. Pour the tea into a pitcher and refrigerate until chilled. Serve over ice.

Nutritional Information per serving:

20 calories, 0g protein,

5g carbohydrates, 0g total fat,

0g fiber, 0mg cholesterol,

0mg sodium, 30mg potassium,

4g sugars, 5 mg phosphorus.

CHAPTER 9:

MORE HEARTIER DINNERS

105. Grilled Chicken with Pesto

Yield: 2 servings | **Prep time**: 10 minutes | **Cook time**: 10 minutes

Ingredients:

- 2 boneless, skinless chicken breasts
- 1 tablespoon olive oil
- 1/4 cup fresh basil leaves
- 1 tablespoon of pine nuts
- 1 garlic clove
- 1 tablespoon lemon juice
- 1/4 teaspoon black pepper

Directions:

1. Preheat the grill to medium heat.

2. In a food processor, blend the basil, pine nuts, garlic, olive oil, lemon juice, and black pepper to create the pesto.

3. Brush the chicken breasts with a bit of the pesto. Grill the chicken for 5-6 minutes on each side, or until fully cooked.

4. Serve the grilled chicken topped with the remaining pesto.

Nutritional Information per serving: 260 calories, 30g protein,

2g carbohydrates, 14g total fat, 1g fiber, 70mg cholesterol, 80mg sodium,

350mg potassium, 0g sugars,

220 mg phosphorus.

106. Beef and Barley Skillet

Yield: 4 servings | **Prep time**: 10 minutes | **Cook time**: 30 minutes

Ingredients:

- 1/2-pound lean ground beef
- 1/2 cup pearl barley
- 2 cups of low-sodium beef broth
- 1/2 cup diced carrots
- 1/2 cup diced onions
- 1 tablespoon olive oil
- 1/4 teaspoon black pepper
- 1/4 teaspoon thyme

Directions:

1. Heat olive oil in a large skillet over medium heat. Add the ground beef and cook until browned, for about 6-8 minutes.

2. Add the diced onions and carrots, and sauté for 5 minutes until softened.

3. Stir in the barley, beef broth, black pepper, and thyme. Bring to a boil, then reduce heat and simmer for 25-30 minutes, or until the barley is tender and the liquid is absorbed.

4. Serve warm.

Nutritional Information per serving: 290 calories, 20g protein,

30g carbohydrates, 10g total fat, 5g fiber, 60mg cholesterol, 100mg sodium, 400mg potassium, 4g sugars,

180 mg phosphorus.

107. Baked Cod with Lemon and Garlic

Yield: 2 servings | **Prep time**: 5 minutes | **Cook time**: 15 minutes

Ingredients:

- 2 cod fillets (4 ounces each)
- 1 tablespoon olive oil
- 2 garlic cloves, minced
- 1 tablespoon lemon juice
- 1/4 teaspoon black pepper

Directions:

1. Preheat the oven to 375°F (190°C). Line a baking sheet with parchment paper.

2. In a small bowl, mix the olive oil, minced garlic, lemon juice, and black pepper.

3. Brush the mixture over both sides of the cod fillets.

4. Place the fillets on the baking sheet and bake for 12-15 minutes, or until the fish flakes easily with a fork.

5. Garnish with fresh parsley if desired and serve with a side of vegetables or quinoa.

Nutritional Information per serving: 180 calories, 25g protein,

1g carbohydrates, 7g total fat, 0g fiber, 55mg cholesterol, 60mg sodium,

450mg potassium, 0g sugars,

200 mg phosphorus

108. Chicken Fajitas (Low Sodium)

Yield: 2 servings | **Prep time**: 10 minutes | **Cook time**: 10 minutes

Ingredients:

- 2 boneless, skinless chicken breasts, sliced into strips
- 1/2 red bell pepper, sliced, 1/2 green bell pepper, sliced
- 1/2 onion, sliced, 1 tablespoon olive oil, 1 teaspoon chili powder
- 1/2 teaspoon cumin, 1/4 teaspoon garlic powder, 1/4 teaspoon black pepper, 4 small low-sodium corn tortillas

Directions:

1. Heat the olive oil in a large skillet over medium heat. Add the chicken strips and cook for 5-6 minutes until browned and cooked through.

2. Add the bell peppers, onion, chili powder, cumin, garlic powder, and black pepper. Sauté for another 5 minutes until the vegetables are tender.

3. Warm the corn tortillas in a separate skillet or microwave. Serve the chicken and vegetables in the tortillas.

Nutritional Information per serving: 300 calories, 25g protein,

28g carbohydrates, 10g total fat, 4g fiber, 65mg cholesterol, 150mg sodium, 400mg potassium, 2g sugars,

250 mg phosphorus

109. Shrimp Scampi (Kidney-Friendly)

Yield: 2 servings | **Prep time**: 5 minutes | **Cook time**: 10 minutes

Ingredients:

- 12 large shrimp, peeled and deveined
- 2 tablespoons of olive oil
- 2 garlic cloves, minced
- 1 tablespoon lemon juice
- 1/4 teaspoon black pepper
- 1 tablespoon fresh parsley, chopped (optional)

Directions:

1. Heat olive oil in a large skillet over medium heat. Add the minced garlic and sauté for 1-2 minutes until fragrant.

2. Add the shrimp to the skillet and cook for 2-3 minutes on each side until pink and fully cooked.

3. Stir in the lemon juice and black pepper, cooking for another minute.

4. Optionally, serve the shrimp over cooked whole wheat pasta, and garnish with fresh parsley.

Nutritional Information per serving: 200 calories, 20g protein,

5g carbohydrates, 12g total fat, 1g fiber, 180mg cholesterol, 60mg sodium, 250mg potassium, 1g sugars,

180 mg phosphorus.

110. Herb-Crusted Chicken Breasts

Yield: 2 servings | **Prep time**: 10 minutes | **Cook time**: 20 minutes

Ingredients:

- 2 boneless, skinless chicken breasts, 1/4 cup of breadcrumbs
- 1 tablespoon olive oil, 1 teaspoon dried oregano
- 1 teaspoon dried thyme, 1/4 teaspoon black pepper

Directions:

1. Preheat the oven to 375°F (190°C). Line a baking sheet with parchment paper.

2. In a small bowl, mix the breadcrumbs, olive oil, oregano, thyme, and black pepper.

3. Coat each chicken breast with the breadcrumb mixture, pressing gently to adhere.

4. Place the chicken breasts on the baking sheet and bake for 20-25 minutes, or until the internal temperature reaches 165°F

5. Garnish with fresh parsley if desired and serve with a side of vegetables.

Nutritional Information per serving: 250 calories, 30g protein,

10g carbohydrates, 10g total fat, 2g fiber, 70mg cholesterol, 80mg sodium,

350mg potassium, 0g sugars,

220 mg phosphorus.

111. Turkey Meatballs with Tomato Sauce

Yield: 4 servings | **Prep time**: 10 minutes | **Cook time**: 20 minutes

Ingredients:

- 1/2-pound ground turkey (lean)
- 1/4 cup plain breadcrumbs (low sodium)
- 1 egg white, 1 garlic clove, minced
- 1/4 teaspoon black pepper, 1/4 teaspoon of oregano
- 1 tablespoon olive oil, 1 cup low-sodium tomato sauce

Directions:

1. In a large bowl, mix the ground turkey, breadcrumbs, egg white, minced garlic, black pepper, and oregano until well combined.

2. Form the mixture into small meatballs.

3. Heat olive oil in a large skillet over medium heat. Add the meatballs and cook for 8-10 minutes, turning occasionally until browned on all sides.

4. Pour the tomato sauce over the meatballs, cover, and simmer for another 10 minutes until the meatballs are fully cooked.

Nutritional Information per serving: 210 calories, 20g protein,

10g carbohydrates, 10g total fat, 2g fiber, 60mg cholesterol, 120mg sodium, 400mg potassium, 3g sugars,

240 mg phosphorus.

112. Stuffed Bell Peppers with Quinoa

Yield: 4 servings | **Prep time**: 10 minutes | **Cook time**: 25 minutes

Ingredients:

- 4 large bell peppers (any color), halved and seeds removed
- 1/2 cup cooked quinoa
- 1/2 cup black beans (rinsed, low sodium)
- 1/4 cup diced tomatoes
- 1 tablespoon olive oil
- 1/4 teaspoon cumin
- 1/4 teaspoon black pepper

Directions:

1. Preheat the oven to 375°F. In a skillet, heat olive oil over medium heat. Add the diced tomatoes, black beans, quinoa, cumin, and black pepper. Cook for 5 minutes, stirring occasionally.

2. Fill each bell pepper in half with the quinoa mixture. Place the stuffed peppers in a baking dish.

3. Cover the dish with foil and bake for 20 minutes. If you use cheese, sprinkle it on top during the last 5 minutes of baking.

Nutritional Information per serving: 230 calories, 10g protein,

35g carbohydrates, 7g total fat, 8g fiber, 0mg cholesterol, 120mg sodium,

550mg potassium, 5g sugars,

200 mg phosphorus.

113. Low-Sodium Stir-Fry with Broccoli and Chicken

Yield: 2 servings | Prep time: 10 minutes | Cook time: 10 minutes

Ingredients:

- 2 boneless, skinless chicken breasts, sliced into strips
- 1 cup broccoli florets
- 1/2 red bell pepper, sliced
- 1 tablespoon olive oil
- 1 tablespoon low-sodium soy sauce. 1 tablespoon rice vinegar
- 1 garlic clove, minced
- 1/4 teaspoon black pepper

Directions:

1. Heat olive oil in a large skillet or wok over medium heat. Add the chicken strips and cook for 5-6 minutes until browned and cooked through.

2. Add the broccoli, bell pepper, garlic, soy sauce, rice vinegar, and black pepper. Stir-fry for another 4-5 minutes until the vegetables are tender but crisp.

3. Serve immediately, optionally with rice or quinoa.

Nutritional Information per serving: 250 calories, 25g protein,

10g carbohydrates, 12g total fat, 4g fiber, 65mg cholesterol, 150mg sodium, 400mg potassium, 2g sugars,

250 mg phosphorus.

114. Grilled Salmon with Herb Butter

Yield: 2 servings | Prep time: 5 minutes | Cook time: 10 minutes

Ingredients:

- 2 salmon fillets (4 ounces each)
- 1 tablespoon olive oil
- 1 tablespoon unsalted butter
- 1 garlic clove, minced
- 1 teaspoon lemon juice
- 1 tablespoon fresh parsley, chopped, 1/4 teaspoon black pepper

Directions:

1. Preheat the grill or a grill pan to medium-high heat.

2. Brush the salmon fillets with olive oil and season with black pepper. Grill the salmon for 4-5 minutes on each side until fully cooked.

3. While the salmon is grilling, melt the butter in a small skillet over medium heat. Add the minced garlic, lemon juice, and parsley, and cook for 1-2 minutes until fragrant.

4. Drizzle the herb butter over the grilled salmon before serving.

Nutritional Information per serving: 290 calories, 26g protein,

1g carbohydrates, 18g total fat, 0g fiber, 70mg cholesterol, 70mg sodium,

500mg potassium, 0g sugars,

350 mg phosphorus.

115. Low-Sodium Vegetable Stir-Fry

Yield: 2 servings | **Prep time**: 10 minutes | **Cook time**: 10 minutes

Ingredients:

- 1 cup broccoli florets
- 1/2 red pepper, sliced, 1/2 zucchini, sliced
- 1 tablespoon olive oil
- 1 tablespoon low-sodium soy sauce, 1 tablespoon rice vinegar
- 1 teaspoon fresh ginger, minced, 1 garlic clove, minced
- 1/4 teaspoon black pepper

Directions:

1. Heat olive oil in a large skillet or wok over medium heat. Add the ginger and garlic, and sauté for 1-2 minutes until fragrant.

2. Add the broccoli, bell pepper, and zucchini. Stir-fry for 5-6 minutes until the vegetables are tender but crisp.

3. Stir in the soy sauce, rice vinegar, and black pepper, and cook for another 2 minutes.

4. Serve immediately.

Nutritional Information per serving: 150 calories, 3g protein,

12g carbohydrates, 9g total fat, 4g fiber, 0mg cholesterol, 100mg sodium,

400mg potassium, 4g sugars,

90 mg phosphorus.

116. Chicken Piccata with Lemon and Capers

Yield: 2 servings | **Prep time**: 10 minutes | **Cook time**: 15 minutes

Ingredients:

- 2 boneless, skinless chicken breasts
- 1 tablespoon olive oil, 1 garlic clove, minced. 1/4 cup low-sodium chicken broth
- 1 tablespoon lemon juice, 1 tablespoon capers (rinsed)
- 1 tablespoon unsalted butter, 1/4 teaspoon black pepper

Directions:

1. Heat olive oil in a skillet over medium heat. Add the chicken breasts and cook for 5-6 minutes on each side until browned and fully cooked.

2. In the same skillet, add the minced garlic and cook for 1 minute until fragrant. Stir in the chicken broth, lemon juice, and capers. Bring the mixture to a simmer and cook for 3-4 minutes.

3. Return the chicken breasts to the skillet and spoon the sauce over the top. Add the butter and cook for another 1-2 minutes.

Nutritional Information per serving: 240 calories, 28g protein,

3g carbohydrates, 12g total fat, 1g fiber, 75mg cholesterol, 150mg sodium, 350mg potassium, 1g sugars,

230 mg phosphorus

Chapter 10:

More Snacks and Sides

117. Low-Sodium Cornbread

Yield: 6 servings | **Prep time**: 10 minutes | **Cook time**: 20 minutes

Ingredients:

- 1 cup of cornmeal, 1/2 cup of whole wheat flour, 1 tablespoon honey, 1 large egg

- 1/2 cup unsweetened almond milk. 1/4 cup unsweetened applesauce

- 1 teaspoon of baking powder, 1/4 teaspoon black pepper

Directions:

1. Preheat the oven to 375°F. Grease an 8-inch square baking dish.

2. In a large bowl, whisk together the cornmeal, flour, baking powder, and black pepper. In a separate bowl, mix the egg, almond milk, applesauce, and honey.

3. Gradually add the wet ingredients to the dry ingredients, stirring until just combined.

4. Pour the batter into the prepared baking dish and bake for 18-20 minutes, until a toothpick inserted into the center comes out clean.

Nutritional Information per serving: 130 calories, 3g protein,

26g carbohydrates, 2g total fat, 2g fiber, 30mg cholesterol, 80mg sodium,

150mg potassium, 6g sugars,

90 mg phosphorus.

118. Kidney-Friendly Egg Salad

Yield: 2 servings | **Prep time**: 10 minutes | **Cook time**: 10 minutes

Ingredients:

- 4 large egg whites, hard-boiled and chopped

- 1/4 cup plain Greek yogurt

- 1 tablespoon Dijon mustard

- 1 tablespoon fresh chives, chopped

- 1/4 teaspoon black pepper

- 2 leaves of lettuce (optional, for serving)

Directions:

1. In a bowl, mix the chopped egg whites, Greek yogurt, Dijon mustard, chives, and black pepper until well combined.

2. Serve the egg salad on lettuce leaves or as a sandwich filling in low-sodium bread.

3. Enjoy it as a light, kidney-friendly snack or lunch option.

Nutritional Information per serving: 100 calories, 15g protein,

5g carbohydrates, 2g total fat, 0g fiber, 0mg cholesterol, 70mg sodium,

100mg potassium, 3g sugars,

50 mg phosphorus.

119. Mashed Cauliflower with Garlic

Yield: 4 servings | **Prep time**: 10 minutes | **Cook time**: 15 minutes

Ingredients:

- 1 medium head of cauliflower, cut into florets
- 2 garlic cloves, minced
- 1 tablespoon olive oil
- 1/4 cup unsweetened almond milk
- 1/4 teaspoon black pepper
- 1 tablespoon fresh parsley, chopped (optional)

Directions:

1. Bring a large pot of water to boil. Add the cauliflower florets and cook for 10-12 minutes, or until tender. Drain and set aside.

2. In a skillet, heat the olive oil over medium heat. Add the minced garlic and sauté for 1-2 minutes until fragrant.

3. Transfer the cooked cauliflower and garlic to a blender or food processor. Add the almond milk and black pepper, and blend until smooth and creamy.

Nutritional Information per serving:

90 calories, 3g protein, 10g carbohydrates, 4g total fat, 4g fiber,

0mg cholesterol, 50mg sodium,

350mg potassium, 2g sugars,

60 mg phosphorus.

120. Low-Sodium Hummus with Cucumber Sticks

Yield: 2 servings | **Prep time**: 5 minutes | **Cook time**: 0 minutes

Ingredients:

- 1/2 cup canned chickpeas, rinsed and drained (low sodium)
- 1 tablespoon tahini
- 1 tablespoon olive oil
- 1 tablespoon lemon juice
- 1/4 teaspoon garlic powder
- 1/4 teaspoon black pepper
- 1 cucumber, sliced into sticks

Directions:

1. In a food processor, blend the chickpeas, tahini, olive oil, lemon juice, garlic powder, and black pepper until smooth. If the hummus is too thick, add a little water to reach your desired consistency.

2. Serve the hummus with cucumber sticks for dipping.

3. Enjoy as a kidney-friendly, low-sodium snack.

Nutritional Information per serving: 160 calories, 4g protein,

14g carbohydrates, 10g total fat, 4g fiber, 0mg cholesterol, 80mg sodium,

200mg potassium, 1g sugars,

80 mg phosphorus.

121. Vegetable Kabobs with Lemon Herb Marinade

Yield: 4 servings | **Prep time**: 10 minutes | **Cook time**: 10 minutes

Ingredients:

- 1 small zucchini, sliced
- 1 red bell pepper, cut into chunks
- 1 yellow bell pepper, cut into chunks
- 1/2 red onion, cut into chunks
- 1 tablespoon olive oil
- 1 tablespoon lemon juice
- 1/2 teaspoon dried oregano
- 1/4 teaspoon black pepper

Directions:

1. In a bowl, whisk together the olive oil, lemon juice, oregano, and black pepper.

2. Thread the zucchini, bell peppers, and onion onto skewers. Brush the vegetables with the lemon herb marinade.

3. Preheat the grill to medium heat and grill the vegetable kabobs for 8-10 minutes, turning occasionally, until the vegetables are tender and slightly charred.

Nutritional Information per serving: 100 calories, 2g protein,

12g carbohydrates, 6g total fat, 3g fiber, 0mg cholesterol, 10mg sodium,

250mg potassium, 5g sugars,

70 mg phosphorus

122. Oven-Baked Zucchini Chips

Yield: 2 servings | **Prep time**: 5 minutes | **Cook time**: 20 minutes

Ingredients:

- 1 medium zucchini, thinly sliced
- 1 tablespoon olive oil
- 1/4 teaspoon garlic powder
- 1/4 teaspoon black pepper

Directions:

1. Preheat the oven to 400°F (200°C) and line a baking sheet with parchment paper.

2. In a bowl, toss the zucchini slices with olive oil, garlic powder, and black pepper until evenly coated.

3. Spread the zucchini slices in a single layer on the baking sheet.

4. Bake for 15-20 minutes, flipping halfway through, until the chips are crispy and golden brown.

5. Serve immediately as a healthy snack or side.

Nutritional Information per serving:

80 calories, 2g protein,

7g carbohydrates, 5g total fat,

2g fiber, 0mg cholesterol, 5mg sodium, 300mg potassium, 2g sugars,

55 mg phosphorus

123. Steamed Asparagus with Lemon Zest

Yield: 2 servings | **Prep time**: 5 minutes | **Cook time**: 5 minutes

Ingredients:

- 1 bunch of asparagus, trimmed
- 1 tablespoon olive oil
- 1 teaspoon lemon zest
- 1/4 teaspoon black pepper

Directions:

1. Bring a pot of water to a boil and steam the asparagus for 4-5 minutes until tender.
2. Remove from heat and drizzle with olive oil.
3. Sprinkle with lemon zest and black pepper.
4. Serve immediately as a light side dish.

Nutritional Information per serving:

80 calories, 3g protein,

7g carbohydrates, 5g total fat, 3g fiber, 0mg cholesterol, 5mg sodium,

300mg potassium, 2g sugars,

45 mg phosphorus

124. Garlic-Roasted Brussels Sprouts

Yield: 4 servings | **Prep time**: 5 minutes | **Cook time**: 20 minutes

Ingredients:

- 2 cups of Brussels sprouts, halved
- 2 tablespoons of olive oil
- 2 garlic cloves, minced
- 1/4 teaspoon black pepper

Directions:

1. Preheat the oven to 400°F (200°C).
2. In a bowl, toss the Brussels sprouts with olive oil, minced garlic, and black pepper.
3. Spread the Brussels sprouts in a single layer on a baking sheet.
4. Roast for 18-20 minutes, turning halfway through, until they are crispy on the outside and tender on the inside.
5. Serve warm.

Nutritional Information per serving:
130 calories, 4g protein,

10g carbohydrates, 9g total fat, 4g fiber, 0mg cholesterol, 5mg sodium,

400mg potassium, 2g sugars,

90 mg phosphorus

125. Grilled Sweet Potato Wedges

Yield: 4 servings | **Prep time**: 10 minutes | **Cook time**: 15 minutes

Ingredients:

- 2 large, sweet potatoes, peeled and cut into wedges
- 2 tablespoons of olive oil
- 1 teaspoon paprika
- 1/4 teaspoon black pepper

Directions:

1. Preheat the grill to medium-high heat.
2. In a bowl, toss the sweet potato wedges with olive oil, paprika, and black pepper.
3. Grill the sweet potato wedges for 10-15 minutes, turning occasionally, until tender and slightly charred.
4. Serve as a side dish or snack.

Nutritional Information per serving: 150 calories, 2g protein,

30g carbohydrates, 5g total fat, 4g fiber, 0mg cholesterol, 10mg sodium,

500mg potassium, 6g sugars,

100 mg phosphorus

126. Fresh Fruit Salad with Mint

Yield: 4 servings | **Prep time**: 10 minutes | **Cook time**: 0 minutes

Ingredients:

- 1 cup strawberries, hulled and sliced
- 1 cup blueberries
- 1 cup pineapple chunks
- 1 kiwi, peeled and sliced
- 1 tablespoon honey (optional)
- 1 tablespoon fresh mint leaves, chopped

Directions:

1. In a large bowl, combine the strawberries, blueberries, pineapple, and kiwi.
2. Drizzle with honey if desired and gently toss to combine.
3. Garnish with chopped mint leaves.
4. Serve immediately for a refreshing and healthy side or dessert.

Nutritional Information per serving:

90 calories, 1g protein,

22g carbohydrates, 0g total fat, 3g fiber, 0mg cholesterol, 0mg sodium,

250mg potassium, 16g sugars,

30 mg phosphorus

CHAPTER 11:

ADDITIONAL DINNER RECIPES

127. Lemon Chicken with Herbs

Yield: 2 servings | **Prep time**: 10 minutes | **Cook time**: 20 minutes

Ingredients:

- 2 boneless, skinless chicken breasts
- 1 tablespoon olive oil, 1 tablespoon lemon juice
- 1 teaspoon dried thyme
- 1 teaspoon dried rosemary
- 1 garlic clove, minced
- 1/4 teaspoon black pepper

Directions:

1. Preheat the oven to 375°F
2. In a small bowl, mix the olive oil, lemon juice, thyme, rosemary, minced garlic, and black pepper.
3. Coat the chicken breasts with the herb mixture and place them in a baking dish.
4. Bake for 20-25 minutes, or until the chicken is fully cooked and the internal temperature reaches 165°F (75°C).
5. Serve warm with a side of roasted vegetables or a salad.

Nutritional Information per serving: 250 calories, 30g protein,

2g carbohydrates, 12g total fat, 1g fiber, 70mg cholesterol, 80mg sodium,

350mg potassium, 0g sugars,

260 mg phosphorus

128. Beef Stir-Fry with Asparagus

Yield: 2 servings | **Prep time**: 10 minutes | **Cook time**: 10 minutes

Ingredients:

- 1/2-pound lean beef strips
- 1 cup asparagus, cut into 2-inch pieces
- 1/2 red bell pepper, sliced
- 1 tablespoon olive oil
- 1 tablespoon low-sodium soy sauce
- 1 tablespoon rice vinegar
- 1 garlic clove, minced
- 1/4 teaspoon black pepper

Directions:

1. Heat olive oil in a large skillet or wok over medium heat. Add the beef strips and cook for 5-6 minutes until brown.
2. Add asparagus, bell pepper, garlic, soy sauce, rice vinegar, and black pepper. Stir-fry for another 4-5 minutes until the vegetables are tender but crisp.
3. Serve immediately, optionally with rice or quinoa.

Nutritional Information per serving: 300 calories, 25g protein,

10g carbohydrates, 15g total fat, 3g fiber, 60mg cholesterol, 150mg sodium, 450mg potassium, 3g sugars,

220 mg phosphorus

129. Chicken and Broccoli Casserole

Yield: 4 servings | **Prep time**: 10 minutes | **Cook time**: 25 minutes

Ingredients:

- 2 boneless, skinless chicken breasts, cooked and shredded
- 2 cups of broccoli florets
- 1/2 cup plain Greek yogurt
- 1/4 cup low-sodium chicken broth
- 1/4 cup shredded low-fat cheddar cheese (optional)
- 1 tablespoon olive oil
- 1/4 teaspoon garlic powder, 1/4 teaspoon black pepper

Directions:

1. Preheat the oven to 375°F
2. In a large bowl, mix the shredded chicken, broccoli, Greek yogurt, chicken broth, garlic powder, and black pepper.
3. Transfer the mixture to a baking dish and sprinkle with shredded cheese if desired.
4. Bake for 20-25 minutes, or until the casserole is heated through and the cheese is melted.

Nutritional Information per serving: 280 calories, 30g protein,

\10g carbohydrates, 10g total fat,

4g fiber, 60mg cholesterol, 150mg sodium, 400mg potassium,

2g sugars, 240 mg phosphorus.

130. Roasted Lamb with Rosemary

Yield: 2 servings | **Prep time**: 10 minutes | **Cook time**: 25 minutes

Ingredients:

- 2 lamb chops
- 1 tablespoon olive oil
- 1 garlic clove, minced
- 1 tablespoon fresh rosemary, chopped
- 1 tablespoon lemon juice
- 1/4 teaspoon black pepper

Directions:

1. Preheat the oven to 400°F (200°C).
2. In a small bowl, mix the olive oil, minced garlic, rosemary, lemon juice, and black pepper.
3. Rub the lamb chops with the herb mixture and place them on a baking sheet.
4. Roast for 20-25 minutes, or until the internal temperature reaches 145°F (63°C) for medium-rare.
5. Serve warm with a side of vegetables or potatoes.

Nutritional Information per serving: 320 calories, 25g protein,

2g carbohydrates, 23g total fat, 1g fiber, 75mg cholesterol, 60mg sodium,

350mg potassium, 0g sugars,

190 mg phosphorus

131. Grilled Pork Chops with Apple Slaw

Yield: 2 servings | **Prep time**: 10 minutes | **Cook time**: 10 minutes

Ingredients:

- 2 boneless pork chops
- 1 tablespoon olive oil
- 1/4 teaspoon black pepper
- 1 apple, thinly sliced
- 1/4 cup shredded carrots
- 1 tablespoon lemon juice, 1 tablespoon olive oil (for the slaw)
- 1/4 teaspoon black pepper

Directions:

1. Preheat the grill or a grill pan to medium-high heat.
2. Brush the pork chops with olive oil and season with black pepper. Grill the pork chops for 4-5 minutes on each side until fully cooked.
3. In a bowl, mix the sliced apples, shredded carrots, lemon juice, olive oil, and black pepper to make the apple slaw.
4. Serve the grilled pork chops with the fresh apple slaw on the side.

Nutritional Information per serving: 320 calories, 28g protein,

15g carbohydrates, 18g total fat, 3g fiber, 80mg cholesterol, 80mg sodium,

400mg potassium, 12g sugars,

230 mg phosphorus

132. Baked Cod with Tomatoes and Basil

Yield: 2 servings | **Prep time**: 5 minutes | **Cook time**: 15 minutes

Ingredients:

- 2 cod fillets (4 ounces each)
- 1 tablespoon olive oil, 1 cup cherry tomatoes, halved
- 1 garlic clove, minced, 1 tablespoon fresh basil, chopped, 1 tablespoon lemon juice
- 1/4 teaspoon black pepper

Directions:

1. Preheat the oven to 375°F (190°C). Line a baking sheet with parchment paper.
2. In a small bowl, mix the olive oil, minced garlic, lemon juice, and black pepper.
3. Place the cod fillets on the baking sheet and scatter the halved cherry tomatoes around them.
4. Brush the cod with the olive oil mixture.
5. Bake for 12-15 minutes, or until the fish flakes easily with a fork.
6. Garnish with fresh basil and serve warmth with vegetables or quinoa.

Nutritional Information per serving: 180 calories, 25g protein,

4g carbohydrates, 7g total fat, 1g fiber, 55mg cholesterol, 60mg sodium,

400mg potassium, 2g sugars,

260 mg phosphorus

133. Stuffed Chicken Breasts with Spinach and Feta

Yield: 2 servings | **Prep time**: 10 minutes | **Cook time**: 20 minutes

Ingredients:

- 2 boneless, skinless chicken breasts, 1/2 cup fresh spinach, chopped
- 1/4 cup crumbled feta cheese
- 1 tablespoon olive oil, 1 garlic clove, minced, 1 tablespoon lemon juice. 1/4 teaspoon black pepper

Directions:

1. Preheat the oven to 375°F Slice a pocket into the side of each chicken breast.In a small bowl, mix the spinach, feta cheese, minced garlic, and black pepper. Stuff the mixture into the chicken breasts and secure with toothpicks.

2. Place the chicken breasts in a baking dish, drizzle with olive oil and lemon juice.

3. Bake for 20-25 minutes, or until the chicken is fully cooked and reaches an internal temperature of 165°F.

Nutritional Information per serving: 270 calories, 30g protein,

4g carbohydrates, 14g total fat, 1g fiber, 80mg cholesterol, 120mg sodium, 350mg potassium, 1g sugars,

250 mg phosphorus

134. Low-Sodium Beef Stroganoff

Yield: 4 servings | **Prep time**: 10 minutes | **Cook time**: 20 minutes

Ingredients:

- 1/2-pound lean beef strips
- 1/2 cup plain Greek yogurt
- 1/4 cup low-sodium beef broth
- 1/2 cup of mushrooms, sliced
- 1 small onion, diced
- 1 garlic clove, minced
- 1 tablespoon olive oil
- 1/4 teaspoon black pepper
- 1/4 teaspoon paprika

Directions:

1. Heat olive oil in a large skillet over medium heat. Add the beef strips and cook for 5-6 minutes until brown.

2. Add the diced onions, mushrooms, and garlic, and sauté for another 5 minutes until the vegetables are tender.

3. Stir in the beef broth, black pepper, and paprika, and cook for another 5 minutes. Remove from heat and stir in the Greek yogurt.

Nutritional Information per serving: 220 calories, 20g protein,

10g carbohydrates, 12g total fat, 2g fiber, 60mg cholesterol, 120mg sodium, 400mg potassium, 3g sugars,

230 mg phosphorus

135. Grilled Vegetables with Quinoa

Yield: 4 servings | **Prep time**: 10 minutes | **Cook time**: 20 minutes

Ingredients:

- 1 cup of quinoa, rinsed
- 1 small zucchini, sliced
- 1 red bell pepper, sliced. 1 yellow bell pepper, sliced
- 1 tablespoon olive oil
- 1 tablespoon of balsamic vinegar
- 1/4 teaspoon black pepper

Directions:

1. Cook the quinoa according to package instructions and set aside.
2. Preheat the grill to medium heat.
3. In a bowl, toss the sliced zucchini and bell peppers with olive oil, balsamic vinegar, and black pepper.
4. Grill the vegetables for 8-10 minutes, turning occasionally, until tender and slightly charred.
5. Serve the grilled vegetables over cooked quinoa, garnished with fresh parsley if desired.

Nutritional Information per serving: 220 calories, 7g protein,

35g carbohydrates, 7g total fat, 5g fiber, 0mg cholesterol, 50mg sodium,

400mg potassium, 6g sugars,

200 mg phosphorus

136. Turkey and Sweet Potato Skillet

Yield: 4 servings | **Prep time**: 10 minutes | **Cook time**: 20 minutes

Ingredients:

- 1/2-pound ground turkey
- 1 large, sweet potato, peeled and diced
- 1/2 cup of onions, diced
- 1 garlic clove, minced
- 1 tablespoon olive oil
- 1/4 teaspoon paprika
- 1/4 teaspoon black pepper

Directions:

1. Heat olive oil in a large skillet over medium heat. Add the ground turkey and cook for 5-6 minutes until browned.
2. Add the diced sweet potato, onions, garlic, paprika, and black pepper. Sauté for another 12-15 minutes, stirring occasionally, until the sweet potato is tender.
3. Garnish with fresh parsley if desired and serve warm.

Nutritional Information per serving: 250 calories, 18g protein,

30g carbohydrates, 10g total fat, 4g fiber, 60mg cholesterol, 100mg sodium, 500mg potassium, 6g sugars,

280 mg phosphorus

137. Shrimp and Zucchini Stir-Fry

Yield: 2 servings | **Prep time**: 10 minutes | **Cook time**: 10 minutes

Ingredients:

- 12 large shrimp, peeled and deveined
- 1 small zucchini, sliced. 1/2 red bell pepper, sliced
- 1 tablespoon of olive oil. 1 garlic clove, minced
- 1 tablespoon low-sodium soy sauce
- 1 tablespoon rice vinegar. 1/4 teaspoon black pepper

Directions:

1. Heat olive oil in a large skillet over medium heat. Add the shrimp and cook for 2-3 minutes on each side until pink and fully cooked. Remove and set aside.

2. In the same skillet, add the zucchini, bell pepper, garlic, soy sauce, rice vinegar, and black pepper. Stir-fry for 5-6 minutes until the vegetables are tender but crisp.

3. Return the shrimp to the skillet and cook for another 1-2 minutes.

Nutritional Information per serving: 220 calories, 20g protein,

8g carbohydrates, 10g total fat, 2g fiber, 180mg cholesterol, 80mg sodium, 300mg potassium, 3g sugars,

170 mg phosphorus

138. Oven-Baked Chicken with Garlic and Lemon

Yield: 2 servings | **Prep time**: 10 minutes | **Cook time**: 25 minutes

Ingredients:

- 2 boneless, skinless chicken breasts
- 1 tablespoon olive oil
- 1 garlic clove, minced
- 1 tablespoon lemon juice
- 1/4 teaspoon black pepper

Directions:

1. Preheat the oven to 375°F (190°C).

2. In a small bowl, mix the olive oil, minced garlic, lemon juice, and black pepper.

3. Place the chicken breasts in a baking dish and brush them with the garlic lemon mixture.

4. Bake for 20-25 minutes, or until the chicken is fully cooked and reaches an internal temperature of 165°F (75°C).

5. Garnish with fresh parsley if desired and serve warm with a side of vegetables.

Nutritional Information per serving: 250 calories, 30g protein,

2g carbohydrates, 12g total fat, 0g fiber, 70mg cholesterol, 80mg sodium,

350mg potassium, 1g sugars,

250 mg phosphorus.

139. Low-Sodium Fruit Tart

Yield: 4 servings | **Prep time**: 10 minutes | **Cook time**: 15 minutes

Ingredients:

- 1/2 cup of almond flour
- 1 tablespoon unsweetened applesauce
- 1 tablespoon honey
- 1/2 cup low-fat Greek yogurt
- 1/2 teaspoon vanilla extract
- 1/2 cup mixed fresh berries (such as strawberries, blueberries, raspberries)

Directions:

1. Preheat the oven to 350°F (175°C).
2. In a small bowl, mix the almond flour, applesauce, and honey to form a dough.
3. Press the dough into a small tart pan or baking dish. Bake for 10-12 minutes until slightly golden. Let's cool.
4. In another bowl, mix the Greek yogurt and vanilla extract. Spread the yogurt mixture evenly over the cooled tart crust.

Nutritional Information per serving:
150 calories, 6g protein,

15g carbohydrates, 8g total fat, 3g fiber, 0mg cholesterol, 15mg sodium,

150mg potassium, 10g sugars,

80 mg phosphorus.

140. Almond Flour Cookies

Yield: 12 cookies | **Prep time**: 10 minutes | **Cook time**: 12 minutes

Ingredients:

- 1 1/2 cups of almond flour
- 1/4 cup of honey
- 1 large egg
- 1 teaspoon vanilla extract
- 1/4 teaspoon baking powder
- 1/4 teaspoon cinnamon

Directions:

1. Preheat the oven to 350°F (175°C) and line a baking sheet with parchment paper.
2. In a bowl, mix the almond flour, honey, egg, vanilla extract, baking powder, and cinnamon until the dough forms.
3. Drop spoonful of the dough onto the prepared baking sheet, flattening them slightly with the back of a spoon.
4. Bake for 10-12 minutes, or until the edges are golden brown. Let's cool before serving.

Nutritional Information per cookie:

90 calories, 3g protein,

8g carbohydrates, 6g total fat, 2g fiber, 20mg cholesterol, 15mg sodium,

60mg potassium, 5g sugars,

70 mg phosphorus

141. Coconut Macaroons

Yield: 12 macaroons | **Prep time**: 5 minutes | **Cook time**: 20 minutes

Ingredients:

- 1 1/2 cups unsweetened shredded coconut
- 2 large egg whites
- 1/4 cup of honey
- 1/2 teaspoon vanilla extract

Directions:

1. Preheat the oven to 325°F (160°C) and line a baking sheet with parchment paper.

2. In a bowl, whisk the egg whites until frothy. Stir in the honey and vanilla extract.

3. Gently fold in the shredded coconut until fully combined.

4. Drop spoonfuls of the mixture onto the prepared baking sheet.

5. Bake for 18-20 minutes, or until the edges are golden brown. Let's cool before serving.

Nutritional Information per macaroon: 80 calories, 1g protein,

8g carbohydrates, 5g total fat, 2g fiber, 0mg cholesterol, 10mg sodium,

50mg potassium, 6g sugars,

50 mg phosphorus.

142. Blueberry Crumble

Yield: 4 servings | **Prep time**: 10 minutes | **Cook time**: 20 minutes

Ingredients:

- 2 cups fresh or frozen blueberries
- 1 tablespoon honey
- 1/4 cup of rolled oats
- 1/4 cup almond flour
- 1 tablespoon olive oil
- 1/2 teaspoon cinnamon

Directions:

1. Preheat the oven to 350°F (175°C).

2. In a small baking dish, mix the blueberries with honey and set aside.

3. In a separate bowl, mix the oats, almond flour, olive oil, and cinnamon until crumbled.

4. Sprinkle the oat mixture over the blueberries.

5. Bake for 18-20 minutes, or until the topping is golden and the blueberries are bubbly. Let cool slightly before serving.

Nutritional Information per serving: 150 calories, 3g protein,

20g carbohydrates, 7g total fat, 4g fiber, 0mg cholesterol, 15mg sodium,

200mg potassium, 12g sugars,

120 mg phosphorus.

143. Raspberry Sorbet

Yield: 4 servings | **Prep time**: 5 minutes | **Cook time**: 0 minutes (freezing time: 4 hours)

Ingredients:

- 2 cups of fresh raspberries
- 1/4 cup of honey (or maple syrup)
- 1 tablespoon lemon juice

Directions:

1. In a blender or food processor, puree the raspberries, honey, and lemon juice until smooth.

2. Strain the mixture through a fine-mesh sieve to remove the seeds.

3. Pour the mixture into a shallow dish and freeze for 4 hours, stirring every hour to break up the ice crystals.

4. Once fully frozen, scoop and serve as a refreshing dessert.

Nutritional Information per serving:

80 calories, 1g protein,

20g carbohydrates, 0g total fat, 4g fiber, 0mg cholesterol, 0mg sodium,

100mg potassium, 15g sugars,

25 mg phosphorus.

144. Banana-Oat Cookies

Yield: 12 cookies | **Prep time**: 5 minutes | **Cook time**: 12 minutes

Ingredients:

- 2 ripe bananas, mashed
- 1 cup rolled oats
- 1/4 cup raisins (optional)
- 1 teaspoon cinnamon

Directions:

1. Preheat the oven to 350°F (175°C) and line a baking sheet with parchment paper.

2. In a bowl, mix the mashed bananas, oats, raisins (if using), and cinnamon until combined.

3. Drop spoonful of the mixture onto the prepared baking sheet.

4. Bake for 10-12 minutes, or until the cookies are golden. Let's cool before serving.

Nutritional Information per cookie:

60 calories, 1g protein,

12g carbohydrates, 1g total fat, 2g fiber, 0mg cholesterol, 0mg sodium,

120mg potassium, 5g sugars,

40 mg phosphorus

145. Low-Sugar Peach Cobbler

Yield: 4 servings | **Prep time**: 10 minutes | **Cook time**: 20 minutes

Ingredients:

- 2 ripe peaches, sliced
- 1/4 cup almond flour
- 1/4 cup of rolled oats
- 1 tablespoon honey
- 1 tablespoon olive oil
- 1/2 teaspoon cinnamon

Directions:

1. Preheat the oven to 350°F (175°C).

2. Place the sliced peaches in a small baking dish.

3. In a bowl, mix the almond flour, oats, honey, olive oil, and cinnamon until crumbled.

4. Sprinkle the oat mixture over the peaches.

5. Bake for 18-20 minutes, or until the topping is golden brown. Serve warm.

Nutritional Information per serving: 140 calories, 2g protein,

22g carbohydrates, 6g total fat, 3g fiber, 0mg cholesterol, 5mg sodium,

250mg potassium, 10g sugars,

60 mg phosphorus.

146. Chocolate-Dipped Strawberries

Yield: 8 servings | **Prep time**: 5 minutes | **Cook time**: 0 minutes

Ingredients:

- 8 large strawberries
- 2 ounces dark chocolate (70% cocoa or higher), melted

Directions:

1. Melt the dark chocolate in a microwave-safe bowl in 30-second intervals, stirring between each until smooth.

2. Dip each strawberry into the melted chocolate, coating about half of the berry.

3. Place the strawberries on a parchment-lined baking sheet and refrigerate for 30 minutes to allow the chocolate to set.

4. Serve chilled.

Nutritional Information per serving:

60 calories, 1g protein,

8g carbohydrates, 3g total fat,

2g fiber, 0mg cholesterol, 0mg sodium, 120mg potassium, 5g sugars,

25 mg phosphorus.

147. Cinnamon Applesauce Cake

Yield: 8 servings | **Prep time**: 10 minutes | **Cook time**: 25 minutes

Ingredients:

- 1 cup whole wheat flour
- 1/2 cup unsweetened applesauce
- 1/4 cup of honey
- 1 large egg, 1 teaspoon cinnamon
- 1 teaspoon of baking powder
- 1/2 teaspoon vanilla extract

Directions:

1. Preheat the oven to 350°F (175°C) and grease an 8-inch square baking dish.
2. In a bowl, mix the flour, applesauce, honey, egg, cinnamon, baking powder, and vanilla extract until well combined.
3. Pour the batter into the prepared dish and spread evenly.
4. Bake for 22-25 minutes, or until a toothpick inserted into the center comes out clean.
5. Let the cake cool before slicing and serving.

Nutritional Information per serving: 120 calories, 3g protein,

25g carbohydrates, 2g total fat, 3g fiber, 20mg cholesterol, 80mg sodium,

100mg potassium, 10g sugars,

75 mg phosphorus.

148. Lemon Shortbread Cookies

Yield: 12 cookies | **Prep time**: 10 minutes | **Cook time**: 12 minutes

Ingredients:

- 1 cup almond flour
- 1/4 cup unsweetened applesauce
- 1 tablespoon honey
- 1 tablespoon lemon zest
- 1/2 teaspoon vanilla extract

Directions:

1. Preheat the oven to 350°F (175°C) and line a baking sheet with parchment paper.
2. In a bowl, mix the almond flour, applesauce, honey, lemon zest, and vanilla extract until the dough forms.
3. Roll the dough into small balls and flatten slightly on the baking sheet.
4. Bake for 10-12 minutes, or until the edges are golden. Let's cool before serving.

Nutritional Information per cookie:

70 calories, 2g protein,

8g carbohydrates, 4g total fat, 1g fiber, 0mg cholesterol, 5mg sodium,

40mg potassium, 5g sugars,

50 mg phosphorus.

149. Chocolate Zucchini Bread

Yield: 8 servings | **Prep time**: 10 minutes | **Cook time**: 30 minutes

Ingredients:

- 1 cup whole wheat flour. 1/4 cup unsweetened cocoa powder, 1/2 cup shredded zucchini

- 1/4 cup of honey, 1 large egg, 1/4 cup unsweetened applesauce, 1 teaspoon of baking powder, 1/2 teaspoon vanilla extract

Directions:

1. Preheat the oven to 350°F and grease a loaf pan. In a bowl, mix the flour, cocoa powder, shredded zucchini, honey, egg, applesauce, baking powder, and vanilla extract.

2. Pour the batter into the prepared loaf pan, bake for 28-30 minutes, or until a toothpick inserted into the center comes out clean.

Nutritional Information per serving: 140 calories, 4g protein,

25g carbohydrates, 3g total fat, 3g fiber, 20mg cholesterol, 80mg sodium,

150mg potassium, 10g sugars,

100 mg phosphorus.

150. Creamy Coconut Pudding

Yield: 4 servings | **Prep time**: 5 minutes | **Cook time**: 0 minutes (refrigeration time: 4 hours)

Ingredients:

- 1 cup unsweetened coconut milk

- 2 tablespoons chia seeds

- 1 tablespoon honey (optional)

- 1/4 teaspoon vanilla extract

- 1/4 cup shredded coconut (optional, for topping)

Directions:

1. In a bowl, whisk together the coconut milk, chia seeds, honey, and vanilla extract.

2. Cover and refrigerate for at least 4 hours, or overnight, until the mixture thickens into a pudding-like consistency.

3. Serve topped with shredded coconut if desired.

Nutritional Information per serving: 160 calories, 3g protein,

15g carbohydrates, 9g total fat, 8g fiber, 0mg cholesterol, 10mg sodium,

150mg potassium, 8g sugars,

100 mg phosphorus.

30 DAYS MEAL PLAN

Day 1 Meal Plan

Meal	Recipe Name	Recipe Number
Breakfast	Low-Sodium Oatmeal with Berries	1
Lunch	Grilled Chicken and Apple Salad	14
Dinner	Baked Lemon Herb Tilapia	27
Snack	Low-Sodium Guacamole with Bell Pepper Sticks	42
Dessert	Vanilla Greek Yogurt with Berries	83

Day 2 Meal Plan

Meal	Recipe Name	Recipe Number
Breakfast	Scrambled Egg Whites with Spinach	2
Lunch	Tuna Salad with Cucumber and Dill	15
Dinner	Garlic-Roasted Pork Tenderloin	31
Snack	Rice Cakes with Peanut Butter	47
Dessert	Blueberry Oatmeal Bars	80

Day 3 Meal Plan

Meal	Recipe Name	Recipe Number
Breakfast	Fluffy Pancakes with Blueberries	3
Lunch	Roasted Vegetable Wraps	16
Dinner	Chicken and Rice Casserole	32
Snack	Fresh Apple Slices with Almond Butter	52
Dessert	Low-Sugar Baked Apple Slices	79

Day 4 Meal Plan

Meal	Recipe Name	Recipe Number
Breakfast	Smoothie Bowls with Low-Potassium Fruits	5
Lunch	Low-Sodium Turkey Lettuce Wraps	18
Dinner	Herb-Crusted Baked Cod	35
Snack	Kidney-Friendly Deviled Eggs	49
Dessert	Coconut Chia Seed Pudding	82

Day 5 Meal Plan

Meal	Recipe Name	Recipe Number
Breakfast	Vegetable Breakfast Muffins	4
Lunch	Roasted Butternut Squash Soup	26
Dinner	Grilled Shrimp with Garlic Butter	38
Snack	Baked Sweet Potato Chips	40
Dessert	Low-Sugar Banana Bread	84

Day 6 Meal Plan

Meal	Recipe Name	Recipe Number
Breakfast	Low-Sodium Breakfast Burrito	7
Lunch	Chicken Salad with Cranberries and Pecans	17
Dinner	Low-Sodium Beef Chili	34
Snack	Quinoa Salad with Apples and Walnuts	43
Dessert	Rice Pudding with Cinnamon	85

Day 7 Meal Plan

Meal	Recipe Name	Recipe Number
Breakfast	Apple Cinnamon Quinoa Porridge	8
Lunch	Kidney-Friendly Lentil Soup	22
Dinner	Spaghetti Squash with Tomato Sauce	37
Snack	Popcorn with Garlic and Herb Seasoning	48
Dessert	Strawberry Sorbet	86

Day 8 Meal Plan

Meal	Recipe Name	Recipe Number
Breakfast	Egg White Frittata with Bell Peppers	9
Lunch	Mediterranean Couscous Salad	23
Dinner	Roasted Turkey with Cranberry Relish	36
Snack	Hummus with Cucumber Slices	41
Dessert	Apple Cinnamon Muffins	87

Day 9 Meal Plan

Meal	Recipe Name	Recipe Number
Breakfast	Cranberry and Apple Chia Pudding	10
Lunch	Low-Sodium Grilled Chicken Tacos	25
Dinner	Baked Lemon Herb Tilapia	27
Snack	Zucchini Fritters	45
Dessert	Lemon Yogurt Parfait	88

Day 10 Meal Plan

Meal	Recipe Name	Recipe Number
Breakfast	Renal-Friendly Breakfast Sandwiches	11
Lunch	Stuffed Bell Peppers with Quinoa	20
Dinner	Grilled Chicken Breast with Herb Sauce	28
Snack	Mango and Cucumber Salsa	51
Dessert	Baked Peaches with Almonds	89

Day 11 Meal Plan

Meal	Recipe Name	Recipe Number
Breakfast	Warm Cinnamon Rice Cereal	12
Lunch	Roasted Vegetable Wraps	16
Dinner	Baked Salmon with Dill and Lemon	30
Snack	Roasted Carrots and Parsnips	46
Dessert	Dark Chocolate Avocado Mousse	90

Day 12 Meal Plan

Meal	Recipe Name	Recipe Number
Breakfast	Greek Yogurt Parfait with Strawberries	13
Lunch	Zucchini Noodle Bowl with Grilled Salmon	21
Dinner	Garlic-Roasted Pork Tenderloin	31
Snack	Low-Sodium Guacamole with Bell Pepper Sticks	42
Dessert	Low-Sugar Peach Cobbler	145

Day 13 Meal Plan

Meal	Recipe Name	Recipe Number
Breakfast	Smoothie Bowls with Low-Potassium Fruits	5
Lunch	Kidney-Friendly Egg Salad	118
Dinner	Herb-Crusted Baked Cod	35
Snack	Baked Sweet Potato Chips	40
Dessert	Cinnamon-Spiced Pear Crisp	81

Day 14 Meal Plan

Meal	Recipe Name	Recipe Number
Breakfast	Low-Sodium Oatmeal with Berries	1
Lunch	Chicken Salad with Cranberries and Pecans	17
Dinner	Beef and Vegetable Stew	57
Snack	Rice Cakes with Peanut Butter	47
Dessert	Chocolate-Dipped Strawberries	146

Day 15 Meal Plan

Meal	Recipe Name	Recipe Number
Breakfast	Scrambled Egg Whites with Spinach	2
Lunch	Kidney-Friendly Lentil Soup	22
Dinner	Spaghetti Squash with Tomato Sauce	37
Snack	Fresh Apple Slices with Almond Butter	52
Dessert	Blueberry Crumble	142

Day 16 Meal Plan

Meal	Recipe Name	Recipe Number
Breakfast	Fluffy Pancakes with Blueberries	3
Lunch	Roasted Butternut Squash Soup	26
Dinner	Chicken and Broccoli Casserole	129
Snack	Kidney-Friendly Deviled Eggs	49
Dessert	Lemon Yogurt Parfait	88

Day 17 Meal Plan

Meal	Recipe Name	Recipe Number
Breakfast	Vegetable Breakfast Muffins	4
Lunch	Low-Sodium Turkey Lettuce Wraps	18
Dinner	Grilled Shrimp with Garlic Butter	38
Snack	Zucchini Fritters	45
Dessert	Raspberry Sorbet	143

Day 18 Meal Plan

Meal	Recipe Name	Recipe Number
Breakfast	Apple Cinnamon Quinoa Porridge	8
Lunch	Tuna Salad with Cucumber and Dill	15
Dinner	Grilled Chicken Breast with Herb Sauce	28
Snack	Quinoa Salad with Apples and Walnuts	43
Dessert	Almond Flour Cookies	140

Day 19 Meal Plan

Meal	Recipe Name	Recipe Number
Breakfast	Egg White Frittata with Bell Peppers	9
Lunch	Mediterranean Couscous Salad	23
Dinner	Roasted Lamb with Rosemary	130
Snack	Popcorn with Garlic and Herb Seasoning	48
Dessert	Creamy Coconut Pudding	150

Day 20 Meal Plan

Meal	Recipe Name	Recipe Number
Breakfast	Cranberry and Apple Chia Pudding	10
Lunch	Chicken Salad with Cranberries and Pecans	17
Dinner	Stuffed Bell Peppers with Quinoa	20
Snack	Mango and Cucumber Salsa	51
Dessert	Coconut Macaroons	141

Day 21 Meal Plan

Meal	Recipe Name	Recipe Number
Breakfast	Greek Yogurt Parfait with Strawberries	13
Lunch	Zucchini Noodle Bowl with Grilled Salmon	21
Dinner	Low-Sodium Beef Stroganoff	134
Snack	Roasted Carrots and Parsnips	46
Dessert	Cinnamon Applesauce Cake	147

Day 22 Meal Plan

Meal	Recipe Name	Recipe Number
Breakfast	Smoothie Bowls with Low-Potassium Fruits	5
Lunch	Low-Sodium Grilled Chicken Tacos	25
Dinner	Turkey and Sweet Potato Skillet	136
Snack	Hummus with Cucumber Slices	41
Dessert	Blueberry Oatmeal Bars	80

Day 23 Meal Plan

Meal	Recipe Name	Recipe Number
Breakfast	Warm Cinnamon Rice Cereal	12
Lunch	Kidney-Friendly Lentil Soup	22
Dinner	Grilled Vegetables with Quinoa	135
Snack	Fresh Apple Slices with Almond Butter	52
Dessert	Low-Sugar Peach Cobbler	145

Day 24 Meal Plan

Meal	Recipe Name	Recipe Number
Breakfast	Scrambled Egg Whites with Spinach	2
Lunch	Roasted Vegetable Wraps	16
Dinner	Oven-Baked Chicken with Garlic and Lemon	138
Snack	Rice Cakes with Peanut Butter	47
Dessert	Chocolate Zucchini Bread	149

Day 25 Meal Plan

Meal	Recipe Name	Recipe Number
Breakfast	Fluffy Pancakes with Blueberries	3
Lunch	Chicken Salad with Cranberries and Pecans	17
Dinner	Grilled Pork Chops with Apple Slaw	131
Snack	Quinoa Salad with Apples and Walnuts	43
Dessert	Dark Chocolate Avocado Mousse	90

Day 26 Meal Plan

Meal	Recipe Name	Recipe Number
Breakfast	Vegetable Breakfast Muffins	4
Lunch	Stuffed Bell Peppers with Quinoa	20
Dinner	Lemon Chicken with Herbs	127
Snack	Kidney-Friendly Deviled Eggs	49
Dessert	Chocolate-Dipped Strawberries	146

Day 27 Meal Plan

Meal	Recipe Name	Recipe Number
Breakfast	Apple Cinnamon Quinoa Porridge	8
Lunch	Mediterranean Couscous Salad	23
Dinner	Beef Stir-Fry with Asparagus	128
Snack	Popcorn with Garlic and Herb Seasoning	48
Dessert	Lemon Shortbread Cookies	148

Day 28 Meal Plan

Meal	Recipe Name	Recipe Number
Breakfast	Egg White Frittata with Bell Peppers	9
Lunch	Zucchini Noodle Bowl with Grilled Salmon	21
Dinner	Roasted Lamb with Rosemary	130
Snack	Zucchini Fritters	45
Dessert	Coconut Macaroons	141

Day 29 Meal Plan

Meal	Recipe Name	Recipe Number
Breakfast	Cranberry and Apple Chia Pudding	10
Lunch	Grilled Chicken and Apple Salad	14
Dinner	Shrimp and Zucchini Stir-Fry	137
Snack	Roasted Carrots and Parsnips	46
Dessert	Banana-Oat Cookies	144

Day 30 Meal Plan

Meal	Recipe Name	Recipe Number
Breakfast	Low-Sodium Oatmeal with Berries	1
Lunch	Chicken Salad with Cranberries and Pecans	17
Dinner	Baked Cod with Tomatoes and Basil	132
Snack	Mango and Cucumber Salsa	51
Dessert	Creamy Coconut Pudding	150

Bonus Chapter:

Holiday Recipes:

1. Baked Turkey with Cranberry Sauce (Low Sodium)

Yield: 4 servings | **Prep time**: 15 minutes | **Cook time**: 1 hour

Ingredients:

- 1 small turkey breast (2-3 pounds)
- 1 tablespoon olive oil
- 1 tablespoon fresh rosemary, chopped
- 1 tablespoon fresh thyme, chopped
- 1/4 teaspoon black pepper
- 1/2 cup fresh cranberries
- 1 tablespoon honey
- 1/4 cup of water

Directions:

1. Preheat the oven to 350°F (175°C).
2. Rub the turkey breast with olive oil, rosemary, thyme, and black pepper. Place the turkey breast in a roasting pan.
3. Bake for 45-60 minutes, or until the internal temperature reaches 165°F (75°C).
4. Meanwhile, in a small saucepan, combine the cranberries, honey, and water. Cook over medium heat for 10 minutes, stirring occasionally, until the cranberries burst, and the sauce thickens.
5. Serve the turkey with the cranberry sauce.

Nutritional Information per serving: 250 calories, 30g protein, 8g carbohydrates, 10g total fat, 1g fiber, 60mg cholesterol, 100mg sodium, 300mg potassium, 6g sugars.

Baked Turkey with Cranberry Sauce (Low Sodium) is a delicious and healthy dish perfect for a special occasion or everyday dinner. This recipe features a small turkey breast seasoned with fresh rosemary, thyme, and black pepper, roasted to perfection in the oven. The turkey is complemented by a homemade cranberry sauce made with fresh cranberries, honey, and water, adding a natural sweetness and tartness to the dish.

The turkey breast is roasted until juicy and tender, while the cranberry sauce simmers on the stovetop, bursting with flavor as the cranberries cook down to create a thick, tangy sauce. This low-sodium recipe is ideal for those looking to enjoy a flavorful meal without excess salt. The meal is not only satisfying but also packed with protein, low in carbohydrates, and contains only 100mg of sodium per serving, making it a heart-healthy option.

2. Holiday Stuffing with Quinoa and Herbs

Yield: 4 servings | **Prep time**: 10 minutes | **Cook time**: 20 minutes

Ingredients:

- 1 cup of quinoa, rinsed
- 1 1/2 cups low-sodium vegetable broth
- 1/4 cup of onions, diced
- 1/4 cup celery, diced
- 1 tablespoon olive oil
- 1 tablespoon fresh parsley, chopped
- 1 teaspoon fresh thyme
- 1/4 teaspoon black pepper

Directions:

1. In a medium pot, bring the vegetable broth to a boil. Add the quinoa, reduce heat, and simmer for 15 minutes or until tender.

2. In a skillet, heat olive oil over medium heat. Sauté the onions and celery for 5-6 minutes until softened.

3. Add the sautéed vegetables, parsley, thyme, and black pepper to the cooked quinoa and stir well.

4. Serve warm as a festive side dish.

Nutritional Information per serving: 180 calories, 6g protein, 25g carbohydrates, 7g total fat, 3g fiber, 0mg cholesterol, 50mg sodium, 400mg potassium, 2g sugars.

Holiday Stuffing with Quinoa and Herbs is a light and flavorful twist on the classic holiday stuffing, perfect for festive meals or any time you want a nutritious side dish. This recipe replaces traditional bread with protein-packed quinoa, which is simmered in low-sodium vegetable broth for added depth of flavor.

The quinoa is mixed with sautéed onions and celery, bringing a savory base to the dish. Fresh herbs like parsley and thyme elevate the stuffing with a fragrant, earthy aroma, while a touch of black pepper adds a mild kick. With its wholesome ingredients and light texture, this stuffing is a delicious and heart-healthy alternative to traditional versions, containing only 50mg of sodium per serving.

Serve it alongside roasted turkey, chicken, or any plant-based main course for a satisfying holiday meal, or enjoy it as a simple, healthy side for any occasion.

3. Kidney-Friendly Sweet Potato Casserole

Yield: 4 servings | **Prep time**: 10 minutes | **Cook time**: 30 minutes

Ingredients:

- 2 large, sweet potatoes, peeled and diced
- 1/4 cup unsweetened almond milk
- 1 tablespoon olive oil
- 1/4 teaspoon cinnamon
- 1/4 teaspoon black pepper
- 1 tablespoon honey (optional)

Directions:

1. Preheat the oven to 375°F (190°C).
2. Boil the sweet potatoes for 10-12 minutes until tender, then drain and mash.
3. Mix the mashed sweet potatoes with almond milk, olive oil, cinnamon, black pepper, and honey (if using).
4. Transfer the mixture to a greased baking dish.
5. Bake for 20 minutes, or until lightly browned on top. Serve warm.

Nutritional Information per serving: 160 calories, 2g protein, 35g carbohydrates, 4g total fat, 5g fiber, 0mg cholesterol, 10mg sodium, 350mg potassium, 10g sugars.

Kidney-Friendly Sweet Potato Casserole is a wholesome, nutrient-rich side dish perfect for those following a kidney-friendly diet. This casserole uses sweet potatoes, which are boiled and mashed to a creamy consistency, and combined with unsweetened almond milk and olive oil to keep it light and heart healthy.

Flavored with a hint of cinnamon and black pepper, this dish has a warm and mildly spiced profile, while a touch of honey (optional) adds a natural sweetness without overwhelming the palate. The casserole is baked to a light golden brown, creating a comforting, smooth texture that's perfect for pairing with savory mains like roasted poultry or grilled vegetables.

Low in sodium and cholesterol-free, this sweet potato casserole is a great option for those looking to enjoy a delicious, kidney-friendly alternative to traditional, heavier side dishes.

4. Pumpkin Soup with Cinnamon

Yield: 4 servings | **Prep time**: 10 minutes | **Cook time**: 20 minutes

Ingredients:

- 2 cups of pumpkin puree
- 2 cups of low-sodium vegetable broth
- 1/2 cup unsweetened almond milk
- 1 tablespoon olive oil
- 1/4 teaspoon cinnamon
- 1/4 teaspoon black pepper
- 1 garlic clove, minced

Directions:

1. In a large pot, heat the olive oil over medium heat. Add the minced garlic and sauté for 1-2 minutes.
2. Stir in the pumpkin puree, vegetable broth, almond milk, cinnamon, and black pepper.
3. Bring the soup to a simmer and cook for 15-20 minutes, stirring occasionally.
4. Serve warm, optionally garnished with a sprinkle of cinnamon.

Nutritional Information per serving: 120 calories, 3g protein, 18g carbohydrates, 5g total fat, 3g fiber, 0mg cholesterol, 30mg sodium, 350mg potassium, 5g sugars.

Pumpkin Soup with Cinnamon is a comforting and creamy dish that combines the natural sweetness of pumpkin with warm, aromatic spices. Perfect for cool weather or as a festive holiday starter, this soup is made with simple, wholesome ingredients like pumpkin puree, low-sodium vegetable broth, and unsweetened almond milk.

The soup is lightly spiced with cinnamon and black pepper, adding a gentle warmth to the rich pumpkin flavor, while sautéed garlic enhances the savory undertones. This recipe offers a smooth, velvety texture with a balance of sweet and savory flavors, making it both nourishing and delicious.

Low in calories and cholesterol-free, this pumpkin soup is not only satisfying but also health-conscious, making it an excellent choice for those seeking a nutritious yet flavorful meal. Serve it warm with an optional sprinkle of cinnamon for an extra touch of coziness.

5. Holiday Salad with Apples and Walnuts

Yield: 4 servings | **Prep time**: 10 minutes | **Cook time**: 0 minutes

Ingredients:

- 4 cups mixed greens
- 1 apple, thinly sliced
- 1/4 cup walnuts, chopped
- 1 tablespoon olive oil
- 1 tablespoon of balsamic vinegar
- 1 teaspoon honey
- 1/4 teaspoon black pepper

Directions:

1. In a large salad bowl, combine the mixed greens, apple slices, and walnuts.
2. In a small bowl, whisk together the olive oil, balsamic vinegar, honey, and black pepper.
3. Drizzle the dressing over the salad and toss to combine.
4. Serve immediately as a fresh, festive side dish.

Nutritional Information per serving: 140 calories, 3g protein, 15g carbohydrates, 8g total fat, 3g fiber, 0mg cholesterol, 5mg sodium, 200mg potassium, 10g sugars.

Holiday Salad with Apples and Walnuts is a refreshing and festive dish that brings together crisp mixed greens, sweet apple slices, and crunchy walnuts for a delightful balance of flavors and textures. This vibrant salad is perfect for holiday gatherings or as a light, healthy side dish for any meal.

The dressing is a simple yet flavorful mix of olive oil, balsamic vinegar, honey, and black pepper, which complements the sweetness of the apples and the rich nuttiness of the walnuts. This salad is easy to prepare, making it a great choice for a quick, no-cook option that's both nutritious and satisfying.

With only 140 calories per serving, it's a heart-healthy dish rich in fiber and healthy fats, making it as nutritious as it is delicious. Serve it immediately to enjoy the fresh crunch and vibrant flavors.

6. Glazed Carrots with Honey

Yield: 4 servings | **Prep time**: 5 minutes | **Cook time**: 15 minutes

Ingredients:

- 2 cups of baby carrots
- 1 tablespoon olive oil
- 1 tablespoon honey
- 1/4 teaspoon cinnamon
- 1/4 teaspoon black pepper

Directions:

1. Bring a pot of water to boil and cook the carrots for 8-10 minutes, or until tender. Drain and set aside.

2. In a large skillet, heat olive oil over medium heat. Add the cooked carrots and sauté for 2-3 minutes.

3. Stir in the honey, cinnamon, and black pepper, cook for another 2 minutes until the carrots are glazed.

4. Serve warm as a festive side dish.

Nutritional Information per serving: 110 calories, 1g protein, 16g carbohydrates, 5g total fat, 4g fiber, 0mg cholesterol, 50mg sodium, 300mg potassium, 9g sugars.

Glazed Carrots with Honey is a simple yet elegant side dish perfect for holiday dinners or special occasions. This recipe transforms tender baby carrots into a sweet and savory treat, enhanced by the rich flavors of honey and cinnamon.

The carrots are first boiled until tender, then sautéed in olive oil before being coated with a delightful glaze of honey, cinnamon, and black pepper. This gives the carrots a warm, festive flavor with just the right amount of sweetness. The subtle spice from the cinnamon and pepper balances the dish, making it a flavorful and healthy addition to any meal.

With only 110 calories per serving, this dish is low in cholesterol and rich in fiber and potassium, making it a nutritious side option that's as satisfying as it is delicious. Serve these glazed carrots warm to highlight their glossy, vibrant appearance and caramelized flavor.

7. Garlic and Herb Roasted Chicken

Yield: 4 servings | **Prep time**: 10 minutes | **Cook time**: 45 minutes

Ingredients:

- 1 whole chicken (3-4 pounds)
- 2 tablespoons of olive oil
- 4 garlic cloves, minced
- 1 tablespoon fresh rosemary, chopped
- 1 tablespoon fresh thyme, chopped
- 1 tablespoon lemon juice
- 1/4 teaspoon black pepper

Directions:

1. Preheat the oven to 375°F (190°C).
2. In a small bowl, mix the olive oil, minced garlic, rosemary, thyme, lemon juice, and black pepper.
3. Rub the mixture all over the chicken, including under the skin.
4. Place the chicken in a roasting pan and roast for 45-60 minutes, or until the internal temperature reaches 165°F (75°C).
5. Let the chicken rest for 10 minutes before carving and serving.

Nutritional Information per serving: 300 calories, 25g protein, 1g carbohydrates, 20g total fat, 1g fiber, 90mg cholesterol, 80mg sodium, 300mg potassium, 0g sugars.

Garlic and Herb Roasted Chicken is a classic and flavorful dish that's perfect for family meals or special occasions. The chicken is infused with the fresh, aromatic flavors of garlic, rosemary, and thyme, along with a hint of lemon that adds a refreshing brightness to the dish.

The recipe begins by rubbing a savory herb and garlic mixture all over the chicken, including under the skin, to ensure a deep, rich flavor. Roasting the chicken at 375°F results in a tender, juicy interior with crispy, golden skin. After roasting for about 45-60 minutes, the chicken is allowed to rest for 10 minutes to let the juices settle, making it easier to carve.

This dish is not only delicious but also a good source of protein with 25g per serving, while being low in carbohydrates. With only 300 calories per serving, it provides a balanced meal option rich in healthy fats, making it a wholesome centerpiece for any dinner table.

8. Festive Cranberry Relish

Yield: 4 servings | **Prep time**: 10 minutes | **Cook time**: 10 minutes

Ingredients:

- 2 cups of fresh cranberries
- 1/4 cup of honey
- 1/2 cup of water
- 1 tablespoon orange zest
- 1 tablespoon fresh orange juice
- 1/4 teaspoon cinnamon

Directions:

1. In a medium saucepan, combine the cranberries, honey, and water. Cook over medium heat for 8-10 minutes, or until the cranberries begin to burst.

2. Stir in the orange zest, orange juice, and cinnamon. Cook for another 2-3 minutes.

3. Remove from heat and let the cranberry relish cool before serving.

4. Serve as a holiday side or topping for turkey or chicken.

Nutritional Information per serving: 80 calories, 0g protein, 20g carbohydrates, 0g total fat, 4g fiber, 0mg cholesterol, 0mg sodium, 100mg potassium, 18g sugars.

Festive Cranberry Relish is a delightful, tangy-sweet side dish that adds vibrant color and flavor to any holiday spread. Made with fresh cranberries, honey, and a touch of orange zest and juice, this relish is both refreshing and rich in seasonal flavors. The cranberries burst open as they cook, creating a natural, tart-sweet sauce, while the cinnamon and orange bring a hint of warmth and brightness.

Perfect for serving alongside roasted turkey, chicken, or as a topping for various holiday dishes, this cranberry relish is quick to prepare, taking just 10 minutes of cooking time. It's a light and flavorful addition to your festive meals with only 80 calories per serving.

9. Kidney-Friendly Apple Pie

Yield: 4 servings | **Prep time**: 15 minutes | **Cook time**: 25 minutes

Ingredients:

- 2 medium apples, peeled and sliced
- 1/4 cup almond flour
- 1 tablespoon honey
- 1/2 teaspoon cinnamon
- 1/4 teaspoon nutmeg
- 1 tablespoon unsweetened applesauce
- 1 tablespoon olive oil

Directions:

1. Preheat the oven to 350°F (175°C) and grease a small pie dish.
2. In a bowl, mix the sliced apples with honey, cinnamon, and nutmeg.
3. In another bowl, mix the almond flour, applesauce, and olive oil to create the crust.
4. Press the crust mixture into the bottom of the pie dish, then layer the apple slices on top.
5. Bake for 20-25 minutes, or until the apples are tender and the crust is golden.
6. Let cool slightly before serving.

Nutritional Information per serving: 150 calories, 2g protein, 22g carbohydrates, 7g total fat, 4g fiber, 0mg cholesterol, 10mg sodium, 200mg potassium, 12g sugars.

Kidney-Friendly Apple Pie is a delicious, low-sodium dessert option perfect for those looking for a lighter version of the traditional pie. This recipe features tender, spiced apples baked with a simple almond flour crust. The natural sweetness of apples is enhanced with honey, cinnamon, and nutmeg, making it a flavorful yet kidney-friendly treat.

With a crust made from almond flour, applesauce, and olive oil, this pie offers a healthier alternative without sacrificing taste. It's baked until the apples are perfectly tender, and the crust is golden, making it a satisfying dessert that's both nutritious and easy to prepare. At only 150 calories per serving, it's a great addition to your dessert table.

10. Pumpkin Spice Muffins

Yield: 6 muffins | **Prep time**: 10 minutes | **Cook time**: 20 minutes

Ingredients:

- 1 cup whole wheat flour
- 1/2 cup pumpkin puree
- 1/4 cup honey
- 1 large egg
- 1/4 cup unsweetened almond milk
- 1 teaspoon cinnamon
- 1/2 teaspoon nutmeg
- 1/2 teaspoon of baking powder
- 1/4 teaspoon vanilla extract

Directions:

1. Preheat the oven to 350°F (175°C) and line a muffin tin with paper liners.
2. In a bowl, mix the flour, pumpkin puree, honey, egg, almond milk, cinnamon, nutmeg, baking powder, and vanilla extract until well combined.
3. Divide the batter evenly among the muffin cups.
4. Bake for 18-20 minutes, or until a toothpick inserted into the center comes out clean.
5. Let the muffins cool before serving.

Nutritional Information per muffin: 120 calories, 3g protein, 22g carbohydrates, 3g total fat, 3g fiber, 20mg cholesterol, 60mg sodium, 150mg potassium, 10g sugars.

Pumpkin Spice Muffins are a cozy, fall-inspired treat, perfect for any time of year. Made with wholesome ingredients like whole wheat flour and pumpkin puree, these muffins are lightly sweetened with honey and flavored with warm spices like cinnamon and nutmeg. The addition of almond milk and vanilla extract adds a subtle richness, while the pumpkin puree keeps the muffins moist and tender.

These muffins are easy to make, requiring just 10 minutes of prep and 20 minutes in the oven. With only 120 calories per muffin, they make for a guilt-free snack or breakfast option, offering a delightful balance of sweetness and spice in every bite.

As we come to the final page of the "Renal Diet Cookbook for Seniors," I hope this journey has been as rewarding for you as it was for me to create. This cookbook was crafted with a deep passion for guiding those facing kidney health challenges through flavorful, nutritious, and easy-to-make meals. Managing kidney health can sometimes feel overwhelming, but my hope is that these recipes have brought clarity, joy, and simplicity to your kitchen.

Each recipe in this collection is more than just a series of steps—it's a gateway to a healthier, more energetic life. The choices you make when cooking hold the potential to greatly impact on your well-being. As you move forward, I encourage you to see these recipes as companions on your health journey, showing you that a renal-friendly diet can be both diverse and delightful.

Feel free to continue exploring and modifying the recipes to suit your taste and dietary needs. Your diet is a key part of managing your kidney health, and with each meal, you're taking positive steps towards improving your overall wellness.

If you ever find yourself seeking new ideas or facing difficulties, remember that you're part of a large, supportive community of individuals working through similar challenges. Reach out, share your experiences, and keep learning—because the path to better health is always evolving.

Thank you for letting this cookbook be a part of your journey. May the meals you create from these pages bring not only health, but also joy and a sense of accomplishment. Here's to meals that nourish both body and spirit.

Wishing your health, happiness, and delicious discoveries ahead,

Baily Lambert

PS Keep an eye out for future editions and updates as we continue to explore and expand the world of rental-friendly cooking. Your journey is ongoing, and so is our commitment to supporting you every step of the way.

Made in United States
Orlando, FL
21 November 2024